D1534731

TO STAND
ON THE
ROCK

TO STAND
ON THE
ROCK

Meditations on
Black Catholic
Identity

Joseph A. Brown, SJ

WIPF & STOCK · Eugene, Oregon

Wipf and Stock Publishers
199 W 8th Ave, Suite 3
Eugene, OR 97401

To Stand on the Rock
Meditations on Black Catholic Identity
By Brown, Joseph A., SJ
Copyright©1998 Orbis Books
ISBN 13: 978-1-61097-568-1
Publication date 6/1/2011
Previously published by Orbis Books, 1998

ELIJAH ROCK

Elijah rock, shout, shout;
Elijah rock, coming up Lord.
Elijah rock, shout, shout;
Elijah rock, coming up Lord.
Elijah, Elijah, Elijah.
Elijah, Elijah, Elijah.

Satan is a liar, and a conjurer too;
if you don't mind out, he'll conjure you.
If I could, I surely would,
stand on the rock where Moses stood.

Elijah rock, shout, shout;
Elijah rock, coming up Lord.
Elijah rock, shout, shout;
Elijah rock, coming up Lord.

Ezekiel said he saw him,
wheel in the middle of a wheel.
John talked about him,
the Book of the Seventh Seal.

Some say the Rose of Sharon,
others say the Prince of Peace.
But I can tell this old world,
He's been a Rock and Shelter to me.

Elijah rock, shout, shout;
Elijah rock, coming up Lord.
Elijah rock, shout, shout;
Elijah rock, coming up Lord.

Contents

Part Two
TO FEAST AT THE WELCOME TABLE

Contents

Introduction

Moses was keeping the flock of his father-in-law Jethro, the priest of Midian; he led his flock beyond the wilderness, and came to Horeb, the mountain of God. There the angel of the Lord appeared to him in a flame of fire out of a bush; he looked, and the bush was blazing, yet it was not consumed. — Exod. 3:1–2

The angel of the Lord in the burning bush: the revelation of the power of God intervening into the most mundane here-and-now imaginable. Moses, we are told, turns aside, to "look at this great sight." When God sees Moses turn aside, God calls to him, informing him that he should remove the sandals from his feet, for where he stands is "holy ground." And "Moses hid his face, for he was afraid to look at God." God's call and the preceding arboreal conflagration are signs of what is meant by *revelation*. The curiosity and conversation undertaken by Moses, and — most importantly — the story he tells after his descent from the top of Horeb, are what we commonly understand *theology* to be.

Theology records a people's response to the truth of God as it is revealed in time. God's truth is real; it has weight, shape, substance. Theology is just as real and can be found in sound and gesture and sensual responses as well as being contained in the thoughts captured in printed words. One poet's delight, "Glory be to God for dappled things," is prefigured — by a millennium — in the rhapsody of another poet, "Sero te amavi, pulcritudo tam antiqua et tam nova, sero te amavi" (Late I have loved you, Beauty so ancient and so new, late I have loved you).

And other poet/mystics still sing, "Jordan river, chilly and cold; chills the body but not the soul." Encounters with God, no matter the time or place, cause eruptions of poetry, art, music, and dance. Theology floats, flies, sings, dances, declaims, and decorates the world, as well as argues for clarity, conviction, and conversion. The beauty of the endeavor of telling the story of the bush that flames with fire is that the storytelling is an act of purification and renewal. We tell the old, old story, and the delight in the act of telling the story is as much a part of the catechesis as is the content of the story. The medium and the message are both sanctified by the encounter.

The issue before us, in these reflections on a theology that is "authentically black and truly Catholic," is to sit awhile in contemplation of the truths hidden behind some all-too-familiar words and signs, to linger awhile in the garden of our imagination and try to see with the eyes of faith and art how the old ones — those men and women of Africa who were named *slaves* and who told Jesus it would be all right if he changed their names — took a twisted version of Christianity and retwisted it into a culture of liberation, transcendence, creativity, and wholeness. What are some of the words we must spend time with, savoring and squeezing and smacking our lips over? African. American. Catholic. Slave. Free. The Communion of Saints.

What are the signs and symbols needing our renewed attention? (For we all have a memory of the old ways and the old treasures. It takes a certain kind of conjuring to get at the secrets, nowadays.) What is it we must look for with our ears and listen for with our eyes? The drums. The dancing. The flying. The singing. Always the singing. The singing, all ways.

How do we begin this process? And why should we, now and again, retreat into the silence of our past — even when we are not sure it is our past, having been told either that all the old ways were left on the shores of Africa before we became American (or European, or Hispanic, or French Creole, or multiracial, or white, or Negro, or all of the above and none of the above) or that our past is an aggregate of heathenish impulses and pagan superstitions, left in the woods and caves and spirit haunts when we joined the "one true Church," whatever sign hung over its door?

We begin by making some grand assumptions that are called (in the high-toned places where learning is sought and paid for dearly) the parameters of our discourse, the methodologies of our research, the tools of our discovery. Many an old lady called these assumptions "mother-wit" and "common sense," but we must earn the right of such naming and claiming. At the end we may say the same; or, simply, "Amen." For now, we must assume the following: Africans, when terrorized by European enslavement, did not, all of them, lose their minds; their sense of established cultural modes of behavior; their adaptive qualities necessary for survival; their strength; their belief in the power of the divine. We must assume that the best and worst of Africa survived the Middle Passage. We must assume that those men and women who chose to survive the journeys into hell that took place over the four hundred years of Atlantic voyages found strategies of survival that they were able to teach their children, and which they taught their children to suppress from the awareness of those who enslaved them. We must assume that those who were called *slaves* knew, rather, that they had been *enslaved* by a formidable group of someones; and they knew that only the most clever could ever hope to be free. We must assume that these Africans were human, desired freedom, and had imaginations which sooner or later overwhelmed much of the psychosis of their enslavement, and which they used to make of themselves, who were not a people, a people whom God would call "beloved" (Rom. 9:25).

Most of our attention will be given to the major western and central African cultures and civilizations which scholars point to as being the major contributors of human beings to the devastation of the Atlantic slave trade. It is impossible to know the extent of the devastation. Speculations as to how many human beings were captured, enslaved, or killed in the "slave trade" vary from ten to sixty million. Basil Davidson offers an estimate of between ten and twelve million. If one were to extrapolate from the suggestion that eighty thousand Africans a year were "captured and exported," then the number could be as high as twenty-four million (marking the time from 1515 to 1820, and allowing for a gradual expansion and eventual decline).[1] Killed; captured; enslaved; found dead on the ships; discovered after suicide; murdered by parents; stillborn; killed en route to plantations: no; we will never know how many lives fed the madness. That void is part of the madness.

As to *how* we shall undertake this journey backward on the circle of discovery, the song "Wade in the Water" can be a compass for our way into African American spirituality. We stride smartly, and with grace, into the swirling, bubbling mix that is history — memory, speculation, storytelling, argument, and assent — expecting a miracle of healing and deliverance. We take the walk of faith, employing all the mystical gifts handed on from generation to generation. We grab whatever comes our way. That is the principle of *appropriation,* well and long practiced by cultures everywhere and kept still as a priority in African cultures throughout the world. We rely on the wisdom of the ancestors, believing that they intended to create a culture that would aid in the survival of the enslaved and the liberation of the oppressed. We seek cultural continuities that survived travel across the oceans, swamps, and auction blocks. We are not afraid of facing the dangers in the water, because some of the disturbances of life come from God, in order to "make all things new."

We take all the time necessary, with each of the treasures of the past. We let the words work their magic. We understand that the creation of art is a religious and a political phenomenon. In the making of art, the culture is taught. We must take the art of the kitchen, of the back porch, of the mourners' bench, of the beauty salon and the barbershop, of the garden and the front stoop, and lift it all up for the blessing of the spirits. And, sometimes, we go back to a favorite theme, idea, story, or refrain, and "sing" it all over again. We take pleasure in the telling of the tale. It brings us joy.

God looked upon all that was created and called it "good." The act of creation (and re-creation) is aesthetic. The acts of giving praise for all that God has created (otherwise known as *liturgy*) must also be understood as having an aesthetic core. We find pleasure in the well-made object. The senses are engaged. The whole person is brought more fully alive in the act of recognizing the goodness of God, and how we are all "wonderfully and fearfully made" (Ps. 139:14).[2] But the act of creation was not completed with the pleasing gaze of God. God set all of creation before the man and woman made in the image of God (complete, inclusive, whole) and sought to know what they would name each created thing. Whatever each created thing was called, "that was its name" (Gen. 2:19).

So the process begins by our wading into the Jordan stream of words — how words were employed, how they were used for the assault on humanity known as enslavement, and how words were reclaimed for freedom and glory. From "slave" and "nigger" to "Anybody ask you who you are (who I am), you tell them you a child of God." On the journey now. To be authentically black and truly Catholic, we are told by the black Catholic bishops of the United States, means that we must remind ourselves that

> the African American cultural heritage is vast and rich. The cultural idiom of American Black people has never been uniform, but has varied according to region and ethos. African, Haitian, Latin and West Indian cultural expressions also continue to this day to nurture the Black American cultural expression.[3]

The writing and reading of *To Stand on the Rock* are seen to be acts of liturgy, as liturgy is understood in the African American cultural tradition and throughout the diaspora. Elements of *call-and-response, repetition, redundancy,* and *personal testimony* will be utilized to give respect to the ancestors and their accomplishments, and to provide instruction for those who are new members of the circle and who wish to learn the old ways so that the children may be allowed to dream dreams of healing and wholeness.

This book is divided into two parts, the first of which will engage the notion of what it means to be "authentically black" (in the words of *What We Have Seen and Heard*). Once the ground of blackness has been surveyed, it will then be possible, in the second part, to discuss some of the issues confronting those who would wish to be "authentically black *and* truly Catholic."[4] To stand on the rock where Moses stood, we must go back to the soil of Africa and climb the mountain of God. To go back, and up, simultaneously, is a journey best accomplished through following the maps provided by our ancestors of the spirituals, the singers-poets-prophets of African American religion who sang:

Meet me, Jesus, meet me; meet me in the middle of the air.
And if these wings should fail me, then bring me another pair.

Part One

JOSHUA FIT THE BATTLE

Prelude

To Sing the Race

You sang not deeds of heroes or of kings;
No chant of bloody war, no exulting paean
Of arms-won triumphs; but your humble strings
You touched in chord with music empyrean.
You sang far better than you knew; the songs
That for your listeners' hungry hearts sufficed
Still live, — but more than this to you belongs:
You sang a race from wood and stone to Christ.

— James Weldon Johnson

The anthropology suggested by James Weldon Johnson in the above epigraph from "O Black and Unknown Bards" reflects an understanding shared by most educated people of Johnson's time and circumstance. W. E. B. Du Bois, in writing about the "sorrow songs" and the Negro Church, asserts similar presumptions about the "primitive" nature of the original African slaves who created African American Christianity:

> What did slavery mean to the African savage? What was his attitude toward the World and Life? What seemed to him good and evil, — God and the Devil? Whither went his longings and strivings, and wherefore were his heart-burnings and disappointments? Answers to such questions can come from a study of Negro religion as a development, through its gradual changes from the heathenism of the Gold Coast to the institutional Negro Church of Chicago.[1]

Du Bois decides upon the radical path of attributing self-consciousness to the *subject* of his musings; yet he does not part company with his contemporaries in naming the subject *savage*. According to the most accomplished critics and scholars writing at the time when these passages were composed (1890s), heathens (pagans, savages) did not have developed civilizations, cultures, religions, or aesthetics. Without culture, there could not be any possibility of sophisticated self-awareness or *intentionality*. Du Bois knows that the savage had a *soul;* therefore a mind. But in ascribing to a theory of the evolution of culture, Du Bois must speculate about the hazy and incomplete philosophical impulses of the savage. There are no systematic records of the impossible: a culture of savages.

The great and glorious accomplishments of the anonymous progenitors of culture must be reverenced, so it was said; but it must be kept in mind that "[they] sang far better than [they] knew." It is often presumed that it is up to those who come at the far end of development — those who are the inheritors of culture, not the originators — to see the complexity of the song, to recognize the gradual changes as they took place over time.

This view has not entirely left the world of African American scholarship and criticism. Even with research into more and more areas of African and African American life and cultural history (especially the reclamation work done for the African cultures that flourished and declined before the beginnings of the Atlantic slave trade); even with the scholarly sophistication of critics who offer methods for uncovering communication and discourse in the making of every conceivable form of African and African American art (from clothing design to hip-hop music), there are still vestiges of the widespread assumption that evolution is much more than a useful biological theory. Far too often it is treated as a fact of cultural development. It is sometimes hard to convince some otherwise well-educated people that there might be a case, in matters of human nature, to be made for "there is nothing new under the sun."

In every time, place, and circumstance, the currently young often think they are more sophisticated, more "developed," than the previously young (their parents, either biological or cultural). The notions of progress and development have become articles of faith in politics, economics, sexuality, and agriculture, as well as in art. An increasing reliance on technology often conditions human beings to look back at the "good old days," with a sense of nostalgia for a lost childhood, a simpler, less complicated world. By common assent, children cannot be adults; that is, they cannot live with an awareness of the consequences of their actions. "When I was a child...I understood as a child, I thought as a child: But when I became a man, I put away childish things. For now we see through a glass, darkly; but then face to face" (1 Cor. 13:11–12).

Even though St. Paul believes that there is an end to the process of growth (heaven), his famous sentiment actually suggests that the "then" of history is always elusive. The future will always bring more clarity, more insight, more stability. Given the nature of maturation, we smile at our limits of the past. It is another issue, though, to look at those adults who have gone before us as if they were children because they existed in a *past* time. How we view the self-conscious intentions of our ancestors has far-reaching consequences for how we view ourselves, and how we see the world of gifts they handed over — or left — to us.[2]

Suppose the black and unknown bards knew exactly what they were doing when they "sang a race...to Christ." Suppose the starting point was not "wood and stone" but a seldom considered and seldom understood theology equal to European Christianity in its richness of detail. Suppose the singers aggressively composed songs to define a company of *heroes* (saints) unlike any found elsewhere in American cultures, but altogether appropriate for instructing a dispossessed and traumatized people in how to "make a way out of no way."

James Weldon Johnson is too much the artist not to be ambivalent in his assessment of the bards' achievements. Later in "O Black and Unknown Bards," he is arrested by the unexplained:

> There is a wide, wide wonder in it all,
> That from degraded rest and servile toil
> The fiery spirit of the seer should call

These simple children of the sun and soil.
O black slave singers, gone, forgot, unfamed,
You — you alone, of all the long, long line
Of those who've sung untaught, unknown, unnamed,
Have stretched out upward, seeking the divine.

Because they are unknown, it is not necessarily the case that they were *untaught* or *simple*. It is this view that locates Johnson, Du Bois, and many who have written since their time in a specific cultural tradition. Not all learning and teaching takes place in an environment of printed books.

To be able to stretch out upward, seeking the divine, one need be schooled primarily in the ways of spirituality and mysticism, taught by a recognized and trusted guide of the spirit. No one will ever know how many "simple" exteriors adorned sophisticated "seers" who could fly off, to be taught by the divine itself; for they remain unnamed. The songs remain as texts to be studied, not just admired and reverenced as objects of wonder. The slave singers were not whipped, maimed, and often killed, only for the subsequent nostalgia of grand- and great-grandchildren, or to provide romantic fodder for the concert halls of Europe and America.

The bards left detailed instructions in survival; they sent their message to the world. They claimed citizenship in a world that would not betray them. They staved off chaos with the power of art. "To make a poet black and bid him sing?" is the enduring and defining question of Countee Cullen.[3] Du Bois (with his own ambivalence) also marveled — as he suggested that the "heathen" had opinions worth the speculation and interpretation:

> I know that these songs are the articulate message of the slave to the world.... They are music of an unhappy people, of the children of disappointment; they tell of death and suffering and unvoiced longing toward a truer world, of misty wanderings and hidden ways.[4]

It is this map to a truer world, the journey to the land of the divine, and some of the messages brought back by the seekers and seers that concern the argument that follows in these pages. Assuming that the slave singers, the black and unknown bards, deliberately and systematically *chose* to sing a race into a truer world when they found themselves across a deep river, a long ways from home, we may be able to read more carefully some of the signs and wonders their artist-children share with the world, as they *write* and perform their messages of misty wanderings and hidden ways; as they go about their renderings of lives behind a series of veils.

Chapter One

Wheels within Wheels: What Ezekiel Saw

The Drum Circle

Many embarrassing and stereotypical judgments have been rendered over the last five hundred or so years concerning the use and prominence of drums in all African societies. Some cultural anthropologists have found a much-needed sophistication and objectivity in recent decades and have corrected some of the assessments of "heathenism" and "jungle primitivism" that had marked far too many travel accounts and were found in far too many purported scientific and theological treatises concerning the many peoples and cultures of the African continent.[1]

And yet there must be granted a certain mythic privilege to the drum, on both sides of the Atlantic. After all, the legal prohibition against the drum in every place where the African enslaved were found in great numbers (and especially where they were counted as the majority) speaks to the inescapable conclusion that the drum did more than keep musical time in the African worlds. Using the reflections of Olaudah Equiano, we can view music and dance as the foundations upon which most, if not all, western African cultures were sustained. Equiano says of his Igbo community:

> We are almost a nation of dancers, musicians, and poets. Every great event, such as a triumphant return from battle, or other cause of public rejoicing, is celebrated in public dances, which are accompanied with songs and music

suited to the occasion. The assembly is separated into four divisions, which dance either apart or in succession, and each with a character peculiar to itself.[2]

To see in a brief and ironic way how the prominence of the drum/dance culture continued on in the Americas, two sources quoted in *Sinful Tunes and Spirituals*, by Dena J. Epstein, will be of immense help to us. The first selection offers an account of the 1739 Stono Rebellion in South Carolina. As evidence of Equiano's description of African ritual being carried over into American concerns, this extended excerpt from the official account of the rebellion is compelling:

> On the 9th day of September last being Sunday which is the day the Planters allow them to work for themselves, Some Angola Negroes assembled, to the number of Twenty; at a place called Stonehow.... Several Negroes joyned them, they calling out Liberty, marched on with Colours displayed, and two Drums beating, pursuing all the white people they met with, and killing Man Woman and Child.... They increased every minute by new Negroes coming to them, so that they were above sixty, some say a hundred, on which they halted in a field, and set to dancing, Singing and beating Drums, to draw more Negroes to them, thinking they were now victorious over the whole Province, having marched ten miles & burnt all before them without opposition.[3]

The ritual aspects of the Stono Rebellion illustrate Equiano's aesthetic understanding of music, dance, and social behavior. The Stono Rebellion and other acts of rebellion and resistance have continued to inhabit the dreams of Americans of European and African descent, to this day — for some as nightmare; for others, as a memory of liberating behavior.[4] It should not be surprising that

> after the Stono insurrection, the colony of South Carolina passed the more stringent Slave Act of 1740; it incorporated many of the provisions of earlier slave acts from the

West Indies, most notably the banning of "wooden swords, and other mischievous and dangerous weapons, or using or keeping of drums, horns or other loud instruments, which may call together, or give sign or notice to one another of their wicked designs or purposes." Classing drums, horns, and other loud instruments with dangerous weapons indicated the fears and suspicions that became associated with African music and dancing.[5]

It is important to know just how unsettling the drum was to those who enslaved Africans and who sought to suppress the public displays of African culture. But it is much more important — of critical importance, actually — to understand how central the drum and its physical culture was to the Africans who found themselves otherwise stripped of all their traditional patterns of security. Within the playing of the drum, and through the dancing that accompanied the music, can be found many of the basic organizing principles of African societies. If those principles were suppressed, then there would be little of Africa left to its kidnapped daughters and sons.

We shall see, however, that through the methods of appropriation, improvisation, and artistic genius, the drum remained, everywhere, and significant African cultural behaviors continued in the "New World," without missing a beat. Robert Farris Thompson and John Miller Chernoff have made valuable contributions to understanding the philosophy to be extracted from the study of western African drum societies. Their articulation of the aesthetics of the drum has been a source of nourishment to the present study. In his ground-breaking article "An Aesthetic of the Cool: West African Dance," Thompson presents the following principles and suggests that a careful reflection on these characteristics might open up larger cultural issues:

Four shared traits of West African music and dance are suggested here, together with a fifth, which, although nonmusical, seems very relevant. These shared characteristics appear to be the following: the dominance of a percussive concept of performance; multiple meter; apart playing and dancing; call-and-response; and finally songs and dances of [allusion and] derision.[6]

With even the most casual reflection, it will be seen that these principles of dance not only survived the Atlantic Crossing but became touchstones by which much of African American cultural behavior might be measured, from domestic and familial interchanges to the latest popular music, hip-hop to gospel.

From the playing of the drum and related musical instruments (the xylophone, the banjo, the clavé, rattles, gourds, etc.) to the dancing and singing and gesturing that respond to the drumming; from the overlapping of the calls and responses (modeled on how the dancers and the drummers interact, which, in turn, is based on how the choir of drummers play against each other's individual responsibilities and signature patterns) to the content of the dances and to the subject matter of the singing and communal commentary upon both the playing and the dancing — the performance style is decidedly *percussive*.

In his development of the aesthetic of the cool, Thompson focuses on a dance performance during which a woman dances while holding on her head a terra cotta sculpture. The goal is for the dancer to maintain her balance, her "coolness." Elaborating upon this and other examples, Thompson says:

> The point of one form of Ibo dancing in Nigeria...is to infuse the upper torso and the head with violent vibrations without losing an overall sense of stability....[M]oreover, despite the ferocity of the "shimmying" of the upper frame, the shuffling feet of the dancer indulge gravity and thus convey balance. When West Africans shuffle — and most of them do in their traditional dancing (although there are dances galore in which dancers, especially men, break the bonds of gravity with special leaps and other gravity-resistant motions) — their bodies are usually bent forward, toward the stabilizing earth. They maintain balance. And balance is cool....It is not difficult to find similar instances of control in other African dances.[7]

The "coolness" mentioned here can become one of the first principles and foundations of an African American philosophy used to stabilize our emerging theology. What has been described in accounts of African dances and in accounts of African American religious services (from Baptist churches in Georgia to Santería in Cuba, Vodou in Haiti, and Candomblé in Brazil) may be better considered as evidence of bodies being used in percussive performances, the final results of which are virtuoso performances of maintaining one's balance no matter how fast, furious, or complex the rhythms thrown at the dancer. It is not hard to see in this rereading of "heathenish rituals" a strategy for surviving the most frightening improvised horrors one could face in the worlds created by the Atlantic slave trade. In addition, how to maintain one's balance in response to unforeseen efforts to "trip" one up would not be an inappropriate lesson for many who were not directly traumatized by the fact of the enslavement of their ancestors. Since such enslavement could not have been the motive for the traditional dances performed throughout western African history, this "coolness" must have been more than merely a *strategy* in the face of slavery — it was a *virtue*, one that survived long after the enslavement.

The drum dance, calling forth such acts of virtue and accomplishment, is a public act. As a public act, and as a representative, mythic act of the community, the dance reflects the circle of what is termed "the Kongo cosmogram"; and, even more, the drum dance is the ritual reenactment of the history of the people. Something now must be said of the philosophical/theological meanings of the rituals of the drum dance, and of the dancers' relationship to the circle they form by their dancing. In *The Four Moments of the Sun*, Thompson writes:

> The simplest ritual space in Kongo consists of a cross written on the earth, the top quadrant indicating God and heaven, the bottom, earth and the world of the ancestors. To stand upon this cross is to swear both on God and the ancestors.

Fu-Kiau wrote: "Man through his initiations follows the sun, because he himself is a second sun." Thus the Kongo cosmogram mirrors the birth of a person, in the rising of the sun; the maximal power in a vertical line which culminates with the sun at noon; the death and decline in the lowering of the sun and its disappearance beneath the sea or earth. Then, when the sun achieves its matching zenith...in the other world, the noon of the dead, it is midnight in our world.[8]

The drum calls forth the people. The people form a circle. The drummers form a choir, calling the people to form an ensemble. The (circular) drums are thereby connected to the people and with them form a stronger circle. The movement of the circle re-creates the journey of the sun, beginning with its (and their) birth in the east. As the sun moves to its full potency, noon, the community establishes its north-south axis of the circle, representing the members' own responsibilities and duties as fully functioning adults. The community salutes the sun in its time of twilight and gives equal honor to the elders of the people, those who have in their care all history, law, and wisdom. The sinking of the sun into the earth (or into the water) is a sign of the same journey all must make into the land of the moon (midnight) — which is believed to be the mirrored face of the sun. Those who sink into the earth are no more dead than is the sun. They, the honored ancestors, are without bodies but possess the full power of the spiritual world and are valued as guides, protectors, and arbiters of communal discernments. Kimpianga Mahaniah also provides pertinent commentary on the role of the cemetery in Kongo civilization:

The cemetery possesses ordering power, for individuals, and for the entire community. When a person is discontent with the conduct of an elder he can always go and complain in the cemetery before the tomb of his uncle or of his father, demanding their support in the conflict which has placed him in adversary relationship with the person of authority.

The cemetery is thus a platform, for it is there that any unhappy individual, afflicted with sorrow, frustration, lack of success, or contradiction, may exteriorize his feelings. And there he regains his sense of self and well-being.[9]

The intervention and concern of the ancestors, the dead-alive who intercede on behalf of those who call upon them in confidence, constitute another more-than-remarkable similarity between traditional Yoruba spirituality and traditional Catholic beliefs. The ritual of describing and calling forth the circle of the community is much like the liturgical practice of locating the assembly within the Communion of Saints. Those who rely on the intercession of the saints should be open-minded toward those who call on the name of the "ancestors" for grace and help. The latter is what makes the cemetery possess "ordering power."

The drums have their own methods of re-creating the community, in its past and present. The master drummers are so designated because they are expected to know the drum patterns and the dancing styles of those who have gone before them. In their long and arduous apprenticeship, drummers are taught to be open to possession by ancestral drummers and dancers, who will bestow upon the questing drummer knowledge of the past; and this drummer must, in turn, bring forth all that has gone before, for the strengthening of the people. All the elders participate in this process. Some are drummers, some are dancers, some are active referees, judging the accuracy of the music and the dance. The drum dance is a public act:

> Symbolically, the drum is the "voice" of the ancestors, those who watch over the moral life of the community, and proper drumming and dance are founded on a sense of respect and gratitude to the ancestors for the continuity of the community which uses music and dance to restructure and refocus its integrity as a source of strength in the lives of its members.[10]

Public acts performed for the moral and spiritual well-being of the community are called *liturgies,* and the Yoruba liturgies

being described here could call us to paraphrase the speculation of Equiano concerning the similarities he discovered — he
called them "analogies" — between the "manners and customs"
of his people (the Igbo) and the Jews. With obvious great humor,
Equiano says:

> The manners and customs of my countrymen and those
> of the Jews, before they reached the Land of Promise,
> and particularly the Patriarchs, while they were yet in that
> pastoral state which is described in Genesis — an analogy
> which alone would induce me to think that the one people
> had sprung from the other.[11]

Of course all liturgies will have common elements, but the
striking similarities in the organization of African and Roman
Catholic liturgies should allow us to be easy in our suggesting
that African American Catholic liturgies may not have to stretch
too far to return to roots which are "authentically black and truly
Catholic." And it may have taken very little convincing for the
Africans exposed to Catholic rituals to adopt (and adapt) what
they saw. What they saw would have been astonishingly familiar.

Joseph Murphy offers a way to speak of the drum-dance liturgies that are being described here, and he also offers a way of
looking at the similarities of African Atlantic rituals. Murphy's
work is a model of how to re-vision the rituals of Africa:

> The theology of the religious traditions of the African di-
> aspora grows out of the encounters between human being
> and spirit in ceremonies. The focus on ceremonial spiritual-
> ity reveals an interdependence of human and spirit. In the
> language of Candomblé and Santería, the spirit is "made"
> by human action. This means that the spirit is made
> present by gestural metaphors, and can be localized or
> "fixed" into physical objects and human bodies. But it also
> suggests that the spirit is manufactured by human action,
> "worked" from more basic spiritual force into the special
> force or personality to be reverenced. . . . A Yoruba prov-

erb states this interdependence most emphatically: "Where there is no human being, there is no divinity."[12]

Ceremonial spirituality shifts our thinking from the traditional Catholic liturgical piety which would have the designated ministers perform the liturgical acts for the benefit of the congregations, whose main function in the services was understood to be acting (mostly or entirely) as passive observers. In this popular way of thinking, designated ministers, furthermore, were fully trained in "gestural metaphors," and at one time in U.S. Catholic church traditions, the severest of sanctions were imposed upon those who did not observe to the letter and to the inch the prescribed liturgical behaviors. The comfort derived from the observance of these gestural metaphors, observed by both actor(s) and audience, is often noticeably lacking from Catholic liturgies in our present era, and this lack seems to fuel the clamor from all sides for "traditional" liturgies. In some ironic way, the hunger is for more "dancing" (ritualized, *gestural* metaphors), albeit for the narrowly and traditionally designated ministers of the rites. Traditionally educated Catholic faithful (those who some would rush to call, pejoratively, "conservative") want, in some sense, to "see" the liturgy ("dance") properly performed, even when there are general proscriptions against "liturgical dance."

But in the African drum-dance traditions being discussed here (and by Joseph Murphy), there are no observers in a ritual that is shaped by — and gives nourishment to — a ceremonial spirituality. Everyone must respond to the drum; each person's involvement will of course depend upon each one's ability and upon the focus of the specific ritual. But everyone dances, and is seen to be dancing. The work of the "spirit" demands the participation of the full circle. As the old song says, "Every time I feel the Spirit moving in my heart I will pray." I have to feel the spirit moving in *my* heart, and I must show the *world* how that spirit compels *me* to pray.

Sooner or later, each must respond to the call of the drum. Not just to let the world know that the spirit is in one's heart, quickening the old dry bones of one's body and soul, but because the focus on the circle called into existence by the drum dance is the still point at the center, the axis point between north and south, east and west, the intersection of private and public life: the crossroads.

In African and African American spirituality, no place is more sacred than the crossroads. It is at the crossroads that the ethical decisions are made, that the visitations of the spirits take place, that the outpouring of the divine power (àshe) occurs. It is in the middle of the circle that each person is challenged to perform the best dance possible, under the scrutiny of the elders and for the edification and instruction of the young. Ceremonial spirituality calls forth *ceremonial living.*

As we read the following words of Chernoff concerning the metaphor of African dancing, we can easily see why a powerful black gospel song would proclaim, "I've got to live the life I sing about in my song." Chernoff suggests that each dancer, in order to contribute to the ritual, not only must dance to the rhythms sounded by one or more of the drummers but must also add "another rhythm, one that is not there." The dancer must, he says, tune the ear "to hidden rhythms, and [dance] to the gaps in the music." Chernoff then expands the dance into the realm of philosophy and theology by asserting:

[Robert Farris] Thompson has described African religions as "danced faiths," in which worship becomes a style of movement that manifests one's relatedness for all to see. As the dance gives visible form to the music, so too does the dance give full and visible articulation to the ethical qualities which work through the music, balance in the disciplined expression of power in relationship.... [T]he notion that one can dance one's faith would tend to lead us in one of two directions, toward an ecstatic freedom of movement that breaks the limitations and boundaries of self and body, or toward a quiet and solemn uniformity of movement that gains power as a community unites to testify a covenant of duty and love.[13]

African Ecstasy

Later on more attention will be paid to the "quiet and solemn uniformity of movement," as it finds favor in the rituals of African American Catholics. At this point, we will turn our attention to the first direction: ecstatic freedom. Drum dancing and the frenzied spirit-possession of its participants have long been the subjects of much romantic analysis. It would be safe to say that every world religion (and quite a few more localized cults) has a place for autohypnotic trance behavior, but, often, one church's mysticism is another's pagan rites, unfortunately. It is to be hoped that the comments of Chernoff and other sensitive students of African religious practices can lead us out of the wilderness of misreading and into a clear perspective of understanding another facet of authentic African religious worship.

The dancer standing at the center of the circle, on the intersecting point of the crossroads, performs the ritual gesture of uniting the past and the present; the material and the spiritual aspects of the world; the power of the divine with the abilities of the human. What is more, the person at the crossroads, the dancer in the midst of the circle, represents creation in its original united state: inclusive, whole. Within each person is the desire to reunite that which has been sundered. The ecstatic moment of traditional African religious rituals has an intended effect which may seem nearly opposite to what is generally understood in the modern European Christian tradition (from the eleventh century on). In such a reading, mystical encounter is described as an "out-of-the-body" experience. Indeed we are told that the great mystics of the Catholic Church, such as Francis of Assisi, Catherine of Siena, and Teresa of Avila, would go to great lengths to describe how their souls longed to leave their fleshly prisons, how the soul hungered for release into the purest and most eternal union with the divine. At the root, though, all our understandings of mysticism are fed by a common truth. As Bernard McGinn says:

I have come to find the term "presence" a more central and useful category for grasping the unifying note in the varieties of Christian mysticism. Thus we can say that the mystical element in Christianity is that part of its belief and practices that concerns the preparation for, the consciousness of, and the reaction to what can be described as the immediate or direct presence of God.[14]

McGinn goes on to offer a reading that may help us directly link our reading of the ecstatic rituals of African dance to the self-awareness of representatives of classic European Christian mysticism:

> [I]t comes as no surprise that union is only one of the host of models, metaphors, or symbols that mystics have employed in their accounts. Many have used it, but few have restricted themselves to it. Among the other major mystical categories are those of contemplation and the vision of God, deification, the birth of the Word in the soul, ecstasy, even perhaps radical obedience to the present divine will. All of these can be conceived of as different but complementary ways of presenting the consciousness of direct presence.[15]

Quite clearly in the same vein, the intention of the traditional ecstatic Yoruba rituals is to provide flesh for the spirit; to make one's being open to the containment of *àshe* (divine power) within the person; even, sometimes, to anchor one of the power-laden ancestors (*orishas*) in the community, with the body of the possessed dancer serving as the anchor. The dancer seeks to receive the power of the divine, for the sake of the community. *Àshe* is defined in a manner surprisingly similar to the traditional Catholic understanding of *grace*. In Thompson's *Flash of the Spirit*, we find this description:

> The Yoruba religion, the worship of various spirits under God, presents a limitless horizon of vivid moral beings, generous yet intimidating. They are the messengers and

embodiments of *àshe,* spiritual command, the power-to-make-things-happen, God's own enabling light rendered accessible to men and women.[16]

Another understanding of the significance of this "life force" may help us to see that nothing is more urgent than to clear western African traditional religious beliefs of the taint of superstition and the unhelpful claim of *animism:*

> *Ase* is given by Olodumare [the traditional name of the Supreme Being of Yoruba belief] to everything — gods, ancestors, spirits, humans, animals, plants, rocks, rivers, and voiced words such as songs, prayers, praises, curses, or even everyday conversations. Existence, according to Yoruba thought, is dependent upon it; it is the power to make things happen and change.[17]

Àshe is the same force found in the Genesis account of creation. It is given to all of creation by the touch of the Creator; by extension all of creation so touched can bestow this power upon other creations. One creates a crossroads through dancing or through guided ascetic practices, such as those endured in rites of passage. Or one becomes an unwilling crossroads when the deified ancestors seek one out through the instigation of others (witchcraft) or through a ritual gone awry. When this power is sought, it is sought for the benefit of all. To dance for the community is to be generous. The gifts one receives are bestowed upon all.

The ethical stance confronts the social good: How does my dancing, my moral behavior, give homage to those who have gone before me (the elders, ancestors) and give protection, security, and instruction to those who will follow me (children, the unborn)? The whole community watches and involves itself in the actions of the individual, and the individual is protected by the presence of the community.

To dance on the crossroads, one must be possessed of much balance and "coolness," and the community has a vital interest in seeing that the calling down of power is done well. This blending of concerns is well described by Dominique Zahan:

> Moral life and mystical life, these two aspects of African spirituality, give it its proper dimensions. They constitute, so to speak, the supreme goal of the African soul, the objective towards which the individual strives with all his energy because he feels his perfection can only be completed and consummated if he masters and surpasses himself through divinity, indeed through the mastery of divinity itself.[18]

Christian monasticism (also a contribution of African spirituality to the world) has much the same intention in its beginning — although with a decidedly contrary method of achieving union and mastery. As we are told in *The Life of St. Anthony:*

> And when they beheld [St. Anthony], they were amazed to see that his body had maintained its former condition, neither fat from lack of exercise, nor emaciated from fasting and combat with demons.... The state of his soul was one of purity, for it was not constricted by grief, nor relaxed by pleasure, nor affected by either laughter or dejection.... He maintained utter equilibrium, like one guided by reason and steadfast in that which accords with nature.[19]

It would seem that the great model of the fathers and mothers of the Egyptian desert impressed his friends with his demonstration of *coolness* and *balance,* achieved after a long period, not of dancing, but of a most Greek-inspired *agon.* Not a dance, but a wrestling match, in other words. The mothers and fathers of the desert exiled themselves from the circle of community in order to achieve their spiritual coolness. Their "dance" of perfection was performed away from all scrutiny. In the African drum-dance culture from which our study draws inspiration, the work of perfection must be done under the guidance of the community, for it is in the community that we will find the *site* of authority. Outside the circle there is no perfection.

In deepening our appreciation for the sense of mystical awareness of the presence of God (*àshe*), we take note of the following
incarnational perspective of African belief systems, a perspective
that would find joyous assent from the likes of Francis of Assisi
and Ignatius of Loyola. Dominique Zahan has this to say about
how traditional African cultures "find God in all things" (or in
Thompson's aesthetic, "see all imbued with *àshe*"):

> Rites which are "obscene" to our eyes may represent man's
> joy in his contact with God. The African may use all of
> the "materials" which his environment puts at his disposal
> in order to express his ideas about God. For him every-
> thing which surrounds him exhibits a sort of transparence
> which allows him to communicate, so to speak, directly
> with heaven. Things and beings are not an obstacle to
> the knowledge of God, rather they constitute signifiers and
> indices which reveal the divine being. Thus a sort of com-
> munication is established between the "high" and the "low"
> by means of intermediary elements.[20]

Much time is given to this alternative view of mysticism because
later on we will look at the cultural continuities involved in the
way African American Christians made use of "intermediary elements" as aids to achieving ecstatic union. It is also important
to see that the traditional western African methods of attaining
mystical awareness would have been directly challenged by modern European understandings of prayer, ritual, and spirituality
in general. This reflection will have a significant bearing on our
discussion, later, as to how African American Catholics participate in modern institutions devoted to monasticism and vowed
religious life.

Finally, Zahan summarizes a style of mysticism which has
nothing of the elitism (and traditional hierarchical suspicions)
surrounding the practices of European mysticism of the modern
Christian era:

> The African attitude toward the supreme being is infinitely
> humble. True, man aspires to become God; certain rites

even lead him there. However, he never leaves his human condition; he does not rise to the sky in order to peacefully bask in the beatific vision. Rather, he obliges God to come to earth, to renew his closeness to man, to descend to him in order to divinize him. Thus the favored place for the African beatific vision remains the earth. This is shown in all the African practices concerning trances and dances of possession, as well as in all the customs involving the ingestion of hallucinogenic substances towards a highly sacred end.[21]

When we undertake our reflection on the African American genius for religious appropriation and adaptation, this observation of Zahan will find remarkable illustration and challenge.

Masks of Revelation

Students of western European art are familiar with the Renaissance and Baroque visualization of the mystical possession and transport of Catholic saints. Holy women and men of God, filled with the Holy Spirit, hover in prayer, just above the ground, or are seen being lifted into more distant, heavenly space. Bodies are elongated or otherwise distorted by rapture; faces glow with interior light sources; the aura (halo) of holiness surrounds the heads of the spiritually favored. And those beings who are closest to God — the wide variety of angels — populate the air, never permitted to touch the profane earth. By the time of Bernini's imagining of the ecstasy of St. Teresa, saints were portrayed as in the throes of something quite close to sexual rapture (representing some of the more disquieting self-descriptions of mystical union, so beloved of undergraduate students, and so much the object of antipathy by puritanic members of various Christian persuasions).[22]

What happens, on the other hand, when eyes so aesthetically trained look for renderings of traditional African spirituality, at least as we have been defining it? We must look at what was most often described by travelers (tourist, military, or missionary) as "fertility dolls" and "idols" and all manner of "graven images"; artifacts devoted to ancestor worship became, in the eyes of the culturally other, masks and figurines used in demonic rituals. And on and on and on. Hundreds of thousands of African artifacts have been removed from their proper environments and translated for European and American audiences as evidence of how primitive animists were desperately in need of the control of civilizing white cultures. While the masks and figurines were being condemned and vilified, they were also becoming valued commodities in the world of art-trading, and were becoming romantic signifiers of all that was dark, forbidding, sensual, earthy, and dangerous for those who would rebel against the increasingly strict parameters of European cultures. Whatever signified "fertility" came to represent the submerged animal state lurking behind the consciousness of the European.

Many museums, even to this day, resort to "fertility" labeling when corroborative knowledge concerning an African (or other "primitive") artifact is lacking. In the field of art criticism, as is true in many other places, relying on one's untutored assumptions may lead one to make projections that are based, all too often, on the common, inherited prejudices concerning the mysterious "other." European discourse concerning the African "primitive" reaches the heights (or depths — depending on one's actual knowledge of African culture and art, I would suppose) in such writers as D. H. Lawrence and Joseph Conrad and (for a variety of reasons) in many of the critics who discuss Picasso's debt to African statuary in his formulations of his cubist style. Presented here are representative quotations which can serve as apt examples of the fervid misreading of African art which has persisted among many otherwise well-educated people. These examples will also be useful as indicators of the tangle that must be unraveled in order to see the statuary and masks for what they truly are: manifestations of human qualities (both good and bad); representations of the great virtues of coolness and balance; and, sometimes, clinical observations of disorders within the individuals and in the community.

From among the many possible selections of Joseph Conrad's

writings dealing with the primitive, semihuman threats to civilization, this famous passage from *Heart of Darkness* will be a more-than-adequate illustration of how the body of the African became a repository of the wildest projections and the basest prejudice:

> And from right to left along the lighted shore moved a wild and gorgeous apparition of a woman.... She walked with measured steps, draped in striped and fringed cloths, treading the earth proudly, with a slight jingle and flash of barbarous ornaments. She carried her head high; her hair was done in the shape of a helmet; she had brass leggings to the knee, brass wire gauntlets to the elbow, a crimson spot on her tawny cheek, innumerable necklaces of glass beads on her neck; bizarre things, charms, gifts of witch-men, that hung about her, glittered and trembled at every step. She must have had the value of several elephant tusks upon her. She was savage and superb, wild-eyed and magnificent; there was something ominous and stately in her deliberate progress. And in the hush that had fallen suddenly upon the whole sorrowful land, the immense wilderness, the colossal body of the fecund and mysterious life seemed to look at her, pensive, as though it had been looking at the image of its own tenebrous and passionate soul.[23]

The study we have undertaken here should make it clear that this woman was anything but "savage." Conrad — whose description sometimes undermines his own judgments — is simply imposing cultural chains of transferred fear and obsession, weighing down both the people and the landscape with his own peculiar sensual needs. In this, Conrad is only the most florid.

D. H. Lawrence seems to have been a student of this passage. In the following text from *Women in Love*, the "superb savage" of Conrad has become the complete object:

> Birkin, white and strangely ghostly, went over to the carved figure of the savage woman in labor. Her nude, protuberant

body crouched in a strange, clutching posture, her hands gripping the ends of the band, above her breast.

"It is art," said Birkin.

"Very beautiful, it's very beautiful," said the Russian.

... Gerald also lifted his eyes to the face of the wooden figure. And his heart contracted.

He saw vividly with his spirit the grey, forward-stretching face of the savage woman, dark and tense, abstracted in utter physical stress. It was a terrible face, void, peaked, abstracted almost into meaninglessness by the weight of the sensation beneath.[24]

The sensation of the observer is what causes the features of the statue to abstract into "meaninglessness." In this passage, the giveaway to the lack of integrity in Lawrence's "reading of the text" of the statue is in the phrase "crouched in a strange, clutching posture." If the figure is truly representing childbirth, why would the posture be at all strange? And, given the great value placed on the birth of children in all African societies, we would have to doubt if the figure's features showed utter physical stress. While authors are allowed to invest any symbols they wish with any meaning they choose, we as readers have an equally jealous right to a subjectivity toward such symbols as is displayed toward other narrative items.

Regarding our last selection, we should provide a certain amount of indulgence for a writer gifted with extraordinary amounts of sense and nonsense in her valuing and devaluing of African and African American culture. Gertrude Stein is an apt interpreter of Picasso's indebtedness to African statues for his inspirations. Picasso's famous portrait of Stein represents her with the distinguishable features of a well-carved Akan statue. What Stein says about African culture in relationship to Picasso is astonishing:

The things that Picasso could see were the things which had their own reality, reality not of things seen but of things that exist. It is difficult to exist alone and not being able to remain alone with things, Picasso first took as a crutch African art and later other things.... [H]e returned [from Spain] and became acquainted with Matisse through whom he came to know African sculpture. After all, one must never forget that African sculpture is not naïve, not at all, it is an art that is very very conventional, based upon tradition and its tradition is a tradition derived from Arab culture. The Arabs created both civilization and culture for the negroes and therefore African art which was naïve and exotic for Matisse was for Picasso, a Spaniard, a thing that was natural, direct and civilised.... [H]e can know Arab things without being seduced, he can repeat African things without being deceived.[25]

But the tradition of visual representation in western African art teaches something radically different from that which is being "read" by the authors just cited. The philosophy that can be refined from a close study of these drum-dance cultures is carved into masks and statues, is woven into cloth, and is stitched into the raiment of ritual dancers and healers. This visual tradition Thompson calls "African art in motion."

We have discussed how symbolic and *sacramental* are the drumming and the dancing. While we will not discuss every area where the aesthetic applies, further attention must be given to the carved faces that so dominate the popular imagination of so many students of African cultures. We focus only on the understanding involved in the idea of masking in these African cultures, briefly contrasting that tradition with the use of masks in European societies, noting a few of the most striking aesthetic differences. Thompson writes:

> A traditional man in Dahomey told me that a person who stands well — and by this he explained positioning enlivened with dignity and power — is born with that power. He made this observation while studying a photograph of a standing image of a woman.... [C]ommanding attitude and presence are ancestral. Received traditions of standing and sitting and other modes of phrasing the body transform the person into art, make his [or her] body

> a metaphor of ethics and aliveness, and ultimately relate
> [them] to the gods.
>   The icons of African art are, therefore, frequently atti-
> tudes...of the body, arranged in groupings which suggest
> a grand equation of stability and reconciliation.[26]

The carved body becomes "a metaphor of ethics and aliveness."
The statues and faces and masks must be carefully arranged so
that balance is achieved between alertness and repose, energy
and stillness, and so on. Stability, reconciliation, and balance
are demanded even of objects that have been shaped for rep-
resentational purposes. And this is not difficult to understand:
all objects are informed, invested, with *àshe,* and their very existence brings power into the environment. Those who make use
of these objects must be careful to keep the power thus contained
in harmony, for the good of the community.

The artifacts are instructional texts, for the edification of the
community. The values of the community are displayed everywhere (as is true in all other classical cultures). High foreheads
denote superior intelligence; kneeling figures suggest the virtues
of humility and generosity; arms placed akimbo on a statue
remind the viewers of the importance of being open to the im-
provisations of the future; the wide, rounded, protruding eyes
memorialize both the virtue and the practitioner of alertness and
curiosity.

The shaped forms, the carved masks, display to the public
view the virtues *embodied within the person,* the virtues that are
held in high esteem and offered as worthy for emulation. This
dynamic might be considered a mild form of the "percussive"
nature of West African culture as it was mentioned earlier. But
what of the even more disquieting forms of masking and carv-
ing, the wildly painted and accoutered distorted masks that seem
alarming to the stranger and often to the devotee alike? These
forms of African portraiture, the subjects of much discussion
about witchcraft and demonism, are, in my estimation, the best
examples of prophetic, "in your face" cultural healing that we
can find in African theology.

One of the worst fates to befall an ancient Hebrew was to be the victim of demon possession, thought to be the result of the sin either of the individual so possessed or of the parents of the demonically possessed. In traditional African societies the same fear is universally considered. The demonic is that which unbalances the individual and, by inevitable extension, the community from which the individual acquires all definition. Some unbalanced, unremembered, dishonored (for any number of reasons) ancestral spirit disrupts the life of the individual by bringing sickness, confusion, aberrant behavior, or some other loss of balance and coolness. The wisest therapists must "uncover" the specific disorder and seek means to restore the lost balance, so that both the individual and the community may find coolness.[27]

The distorted, "hot" masks are used as mirrors, in other words, allowing the person — or the group — so demonically charged to see the disorder within and gain control of the disruptive spirit. This becomes a vivid example of several elements of Thompson's "aesthetic of the cool." To dance the very picture of the demonic spirit "in its face," as it were, is to participate in a percussive performance style; to work for the restoration of the inner pulse that guides the individual to a restoration of balance; to engage in songs and dances of allusion and derision, by performing dances that directly challenge — if not blatantly ridicule — the out-of-control element of the community. Public shame and ridicule are given a high priority in African communities (on the continent and in diaspora) as techniques for maintaining ethical control over the behavior of all the members of a society. To play one's faults in front of one is a sure way, it is thought, to bring the errant individual back to the "correct" beat.

The masks reveal that which is within. The calm, serene masks that delight even the most untutored eyes achieve that coolness and serenity by providing contrasting shapes and forms to reinforce the tension of coolness, either in an individual piece or in a grouping. The distorted, wildly active masks also show a picture of what is inside — with the intention of providing a challenge to distorted behavior and providing cautionary instruction of how not to look, of what to avoid, of what to fear inside one's self.

This tradition of wearing a mask, of presenting a picture of the inner reality, is, of course, in direct and enduring contrast with the European mode of using masks to avoid responsibility, accountability, or disclosure. From the revelers of medieval carnivals to the characters in operas from the likes of Mozart and Richard Strauss, the protection of the mask is a commonplace in European costume. African secret societies wear masks to reinforce the power of the virtues (or defects) they are demonstrating to the public. The text is more important than the wearer, in this context. For the masked European, the text is ambiguous, untrustworthy, and disruptive for all who encounter it. The intention is to deceive, never to instruct.

We shall have further recourse to how masks have been used by these different cultures when we look at some of the implications of the conflicts that erupted when European cultures violated the sacred circles of African societies and destroyed the ground upon which the African stood (and danced), distorted the very face of humanity for the Africans, brought the concept of death to the veneration of ancestors, and destroyed the healing power of cultural history.

When the circle was destroyed, the demons were let loose. The struggle for African American religious activity was (and still is) to restore a sense of the circle of the cosmos; to aggressively confront the demons that threatened to wreak spiritual and physical destruction upon all the enslaved; and to learn the proper names of the spirits that haunted the world in which the enslaved found themselves.

Been in the Storm So Long

"And out of the ground the Lord God formed
every beast of the field,
and every fowl of the air; and brought them unto Adam
to see what he would call them: and whatsoever Adam
  called
every living creature, that was the name thereof.

                                        "And Adam
gave names to all cattle, and to the fowl of the air,
and to every beast of the field;
but for Adam there was not found
an help meet for him."

And there never will be, not as long as Adam
names more than the beasts of the fields
the fowl of the air
                  the fish that fill the oceans.

And what shall we call them   children
And what shall we call them   elders

mother and father   and   sister and brother

no

we shall call them creatures
for we must have dominion over them
for we must name and subdue them
for they are the color of the earth

they are fertile and warm and absorbing of the blood and
    tears
we shed
            and we are afraid of that which is strong and
    has no
end
        we must subdue our fear

let no man NO WOMAN have dominion over my tongue

for I am Adam
the only man
only the man
only man

there is no help meet

and I must not name my fear

who would be woman would be child would be
sister brother
friend lover
help meet
never

no one remembers the beginning
so the story can never be told true
name that the first sin:

the memory of our beginning was taken from us

we must imagine there were children at play
on the edge of the forest on the edge of the ocean on the
    edge
of the world

we must imagine that the house that moved among the
    waters
stunned all who saw it
earth that moves upon the sea

men who are the color of moonlight must come from
   the homes of the ancestors   we must honor them as
   returning to give us blessing

prepare to greet the men the color of moonlight
offer them food   offer them wine and rest and necklaces of
   gold
garlands of cowry shells

offer them your dreams child
offer the child of your beginning and your ending
the edge of the world is sheer and unforgiving
the edge of the world can kill

we called them men from the world of the moonlight
they called me animal   they killed my father as he ran to
   save me

name that the second sin:
adam was ashamed and lied

"We are almost a nation of dancers, musicians, and poets.
Every great event, such as a triumphant return from battle,
or other cause of public rejoicing, is celebrated in public
dances, which are accompanied with songs and music
suited to the occasion."   —Olaudah Equiano, 1792

By the waters of Babylon where we sat down,
and where we wept   when we remembered Zion.
Oh, the wicked carry us away to captivity
required of us a song.
How can we sing our holy song in a strange land?

What song can suit the cutting away the foundation of the
   world?
And we wanted only to feast the men the color of moonlight

"Now the serpent was more subtil than any beast of the field
which the Lord God had made."

"On being brought on board, says Dr. Trotter, they show signs of *extreme distress and despair, from a feeling of their situation, and regret at being torn from their friends and connections;* many retain those impressions for a long time; in proof of which, the slaves on board his ship being often heard in the night, making a howling melancholy noise, expressive of extreme anguish, he repeatedly ordered the woman, who had been his interpreter, to inquire into the cause. She discovered it to be owing to their having dreamt they were in *their own country again,* and finding themselves when awake, *in the hold of a slave ship.* This exquisite sensibility was particularly observable among the women, many of whom, on such occasions, he found in hysteric fits."

—Testimony before House of Commons, 1790–91

We are
almost
a nation of dancers, musicians, and poets

we are
almost

human

howling melancholy
into the pitiless night

giving birth to children who will weep
to live
who will never
live thus

while the wicked carry us away
captivity

[one old man speaks of his last day as a child]

it was my king who sold me to the traders

at
Gorée   Elmina

The Arab trader came into our village one afternoon
to visit with the father of his brother's wife
who instructed the young boys in the ways of Muhammad
and the wisdom found in the Qur'an.

The boys of my village — those of us who had not yet gone
on the manhood journey — were sent to the place where
we grew and harvested the ba-koko. It was early in the
season for such work, but we used the time for a holiday
of walking singing and playing warrior on the hunt.

They came for us, the guard of the king. They came for
us out of the trees. They put the ropes around our necks
and took us to the shore where the small boats were waiting. Five of the boats took us to the larger boat out on
the water. The Arab trader stood talking with the father of
his brother's wife and the uncle of the king. Our teacher
did not look at us. He would not take our message to our
mothers. He would not give us a word for the journey. Al-
lah will not be praised with these lips. Never more praise
from these lips.

He would call us the sons of the prophets
Muhammad's little soldiers
He would call us his children
He would not look at us as the brother of his daughter's
    husband
put us into the dark box upon the deck of his boat.

Later that night
the Arab trader came to the place where we were tied
He called me a whimpering dog
He brought me to the floor of the boat and put his weight
upon my back
He pushed into me like a knife and he called me
a whimpering dog

Never more praise from these lips.
What does a word mean when I have been twisted
into the shape of a dog and bitten
in my soul with such a knife of flesh as that carried
by the trader of slaves who slept in my village?

Deep River
my home is over Jordan

Oh what a wide and deep
deep
River

"Upon placing beside the heads of the Negro and the Cal-
muck those of the European and the ape, I perceived that
a line drawn from the forehead to the upper lip indicates a
difference in the physiognomy of these peoples and makes
apparent a marked analogy between the head of the Negro and that of the ape. After having traced the outline
of several of these heads on a horizontal line, I added the
facial lines of the faces, with their different angles; and
immediately upon inclining the facial line forward, I obtained a head like that of the ancients; but when I inclined
that line backwards, I produced a Negro physiognomy, and
definitively the profile of an ape, of a Chinese, of an idiot
in proportion as I inclined this same line more or less to
the rear."   —Petrus Camper, *Dissertation*, 1791

"Deformity is indeed unknown amongst us. I mean that of
shape. Numbers of the natives of Eboe, now in London,
might be brought in support of this assertion: for, in regard
to complexion, ideas of beauty are wholly relative. I remember while in Africa to have seen three negro children,
who were tawny, and another quite white, who were universally regarded as deformed by myself and the natives in
general, as far as related to their complexions. Our women

too, were, in my eyes at least, uncommonly graceful, alert,
and modest to a degree of bashfulness."

—Olaudah Equiano, 1792

anybody ask you
who you are
who
you are
who you are
anybody ask you who you are

tell them:
I'm a child of God

a long ways from home

a long ways from home

we knew how to cultivate the rice they set us to growing
we learned the care of the cattle
we found ways to comfort the children
hold the weary and the lonely

we took the earth we stood upon and poured our
salty water and our blood
                              and sometimes our aching milkseed

upon it

we will bury ourselves here
we will be the ancestors of sorrow
for our children
be the bones of divination
be the forest of spirits
be the beginning again

of the people

we will
BE

claim this your Eden?
that is the lie

claim this your Jerusalem?
that is the lie

claim us and our children
that is the breaking of the oath
between you and the god you made in your image

even false gods will burn for their jealous privilege
you will walk among the trees of the woods and hear
the murmuring

the whispering stars will spit upon your eyelids

you will bear the curse of blindness

you do not see your hunger upon my flesh

you do not see your fear upon my back

you do not see my bitterness in my kiss

you do not recognize our children in the yard

my voice has been captured by the iron pot in the prayer
    grove
I am unfit for your service
I am unfit by your own reckoning

I am your reckoning

Indeed
I tremble for my country when I consider that God
is just:

that his justice cannot sleep for ever:
that considering numbers, nature, and natural means only,
a revolution of the wheel of fortune, an exchange of
    situation,

is among possible events:

that it may become probable by supernatural interference!

The Almighty has no attribute which can take side with us
in such a contest.
                    —Thomas Jefferson, *Notes on the State of Virginia,* 1782

Go down Moses   Way down in Egypt land   Tell old
Pharaoh To let my people go.   Didn't my Lord deliver
Daniel Daniel   Didn't my Lord deliver Daniel   Then
why not
every
man woman child among us and yet to come?

There's no hiding place down here
Oh, I went to the rock to hide my face
Rock cried out
"No hiding place"
There's
no
hiding place down
here

O the blind man stood on the road and cried

Any how anyhow anyhow my lord Anyhow yes, anyhow
I'm going up to heaven anyhow.
If your brother talk about you
And scandalize your name
Down at the cross
you must bow.
I'm going up to heaven anyhow.

While the blind stand on the road and cry

"The simplest ritual space in the Kongo consists of a cross
written on the earth, the top quadrant indicating God and
heaven, the bottom, earth and the world of the ancestors.

To stand upon this cross is to swear both on God and the
ancestors."   — Robert Farris Thompson, 1981

"To use his own words, further, he said, 'If you give a nigger an inch, he will take an ell. A nigger should know
nothing but to obey his master — to do as he is told to do.
Learning would *spoil* the best nigger in the world. Now,'
said he, 'if you teach that nigger (speaking of myself) how
to read, there would be no keeping him. It would forever
unfit him to be a slave. He would at once become unman-
ageable, and of no value to his master. As to himself, it
could do him no good, but a great deal of harm. It would
make him discontented and unhappy.' From that moment,
I understood the pathway from slavery to freedom. It was
just what I wanted. . . . What he most dreaded, that I most
desired. What he most loved, that I most hated. That
which to him was a great evil, to be carefully shunned,
was to me a great good, to be diligently sought; and the
argument which he so warmly urged, against my learning to read, only served to inspire me with a desire and
a determination to learn."   — Frederick Douglass, 1845

Speaking of myself
of myself
master
of myself
"that nigger" will learn to
read
to speak
of and for

my very
black
self
your words are captured roped into the corral of my self
to be used to cut into your back

speaking of myself
I call myself before me
in the garden of God

and name myself not Adam not Eve but Self the Child
   of God

Chapter Two

How Does It Feel
to Come Out the Wilderness?

It was religion which sent the American Founding Fathers on their initial "errand into the wilderness," an event which subsequently required the involuntary relocation of millions of Africans to make that errand viable. — C. Eric Lincoln

The west India planters prefer the slaves of Benin or Eboe, to those of any part of Guinea, for their hardiness, intelligence, integrity, and zeal. — Those benefits are felt by us in the general healthiness of the people, and in their vigour and activity; I might have added, too, to their comeliness.
— Olaudah Equiano

The Face of the Deep

The dislocation and relocation of the millions of Africans referred to in the above epigraphs did much more than move human beings from one piece of land to another, for whatever form of servitude. The *leaving of the land,* as an act in itself, served to sunder the cosmos of the Africans thus uprooted. Unlike many of the "expatriates" of Europe — some of whom fled persecutions, others of whom were willing and eager co-creators of their new fates and for whom there was little nostalgia for actual plots of land — the Africans suffered singularly real and permanent trauma in that the concept of *ancestral land* was not abstract but a lived experience upon which all notions of culture were grounded. The mental health of these Africans who

49

were involuntarily relocated had always depended on recognizing a universe that was, literally, based upon the bones of their
ancestors.

When the relocation took place, the beginning and end point
of their human — African — existence was obliterated. This
philosophical destruction is seldom highlighted in studies of slavery, though myriad examples of the result of this upheaval of
meaning are recorded, especially in accounts concerning the newly
enslaved who either morosely or enthusiastically committed suicide rather than remain on board the slave ships. Vincent Harding
collects testimony pertinent to this point in *There Is a River:*

> When we are slaved and out at Sea, it is commonly imag-
> ined, the Negroes ignorance of Navigation, will always be
> a safeguard; yet, as many of them think themselves bought
> to eat, and more, *that Death will send them into their own
> Country,* there has not been wanting Examples of rising
> and killing a Ship's Company, distant from land.[1]

And, further, one widely circulated account of a mass suicide
states:

> On the French ship *Le Rodeur,* which had left Bonny Town
> on the Guinea Coast and was several days at sea, there was
> a sudden commotion. The Africans began charging across
> the decks in every direction. Eluding the flailing arms of
> the crew, avoiding the nettings, they hurled themselves into
> the ocean. An eyewitness later wrote: "The Negroes . . . who
> had got off, continued dancing about the waves, yelling
> with all their might, what seemed to me a song of triumph
> and they were soon joined by several of their companions
> still on deck."[2]

Since slavery was not new to Africa, and there were even
western African proverbs suggesting appropriate behavior for
slaves, the element of suicide as a response to bondage must
be judged as a new phenomenon, accompanying the utterly new
form of slavery introduced by the Europeans. The travel by water

terrified; this was not slavery on the same, *familiar,* land. Resisting to the point of death; ritualizing the resistance; and locking the struggle forever in the imagination of the observers: these acts challenge the picture of tragic submission to the dehumanization of slavery, a picture which leads inevitably to an art form that would be defined, perhaps too simply and too often, as "sorrow songs." From such accounts as these, the power-laden images found in such songs as "Deep River" take on added layers of meaning: "I want to cross over into camp ground [or 'homeland']." Those singers who asserted that their home was "over Jordan" may have meant even more than some astute critics have realized.[3] Choosing physical death over alienation from the land of their birth — in their minds the only appropriate final resting place — gave these women and men a sense of freedom that moved unchallenged throughout the history of African American singing and art. "And before I'd be a slave, I'll be buried in my grave / and go home to my Lord and be free." "Ain't gonna let nobody turn me 'round, turn me 'round, turn me 'round. . . . "

If one scans over a typography which appears to us, today, as woefully and condescendingly tied to a specific time in American history, the following insight gathered by Howard Odum and Guy Johnson is rich with confirmation:

> The "big fish" or "sherk" represents the terror of the sea to the Negro. One old man explained this fact by saying that it was because the Negroes were terrified as they were brought over from Africa, that they "saw de whales and de fishes in de sea," and that "de race hain't nebber got over it yet."[4]

Of the many suicides Vincent Harding says:

> These forerunners who fought and sang, who starved themselves to death in the darkness of the ships' holds, have forced their way into the ever-flowing river of black struggle. To call such acts "passive resistance" is to deny the vast realms of the spirit, to count resistance only by its

outward physical modes.... Their form of resistance again challenged and denied the ultimate authority of the white traders over their lives and their spirits.... [Making this radical break, these men and women] took charge of their future, joining it with their own past.[5]

And the race "ain't never got over it" yet. Taking "charge of their future [and] joining it with their own past" is exactly what these forerunners intended. They had to return somehow to the community of their ancestors. African resistance to slavery, witnessed by the surviving companions on the decks of slave ships and also seen and deeply felt by the slavers' crews, gives rise to songs of defiance and sorrow, independence and transcendence — even while on the journey over the water.

It is in the songs that we shall find the keys to unlocking the treasure of African American theology and culture that will inform the rest of the study undertaken here. While the sacred music of African Americans has been a fountain of much enduring wisdom and enlightenment over the last 150 years, there are still foundational issues of black theology to be explored — especially in the realms of spirituality, liturgy, and catechetics, areas of much natural concern to black Catholics. More than apt illustrations of traditional theological arguments and categories (the use to which the songs are often put), black sacred songs must be the starting point of African American theology, the very structure of the songs informing the theology that is constructed from the "black experience." That experience is active, creative, sophisticated, and carries an inheritance from many West African cultures. As James Cone has said:

To interpret the theological significance of ["Every Time I Feel the Spirit"] for the black community, "academic" tools are not enough. The interpreter must *feel* the Spirit; that is, he must feel his way into the power of black music, responding to both its rhythm and the faith in experience it affirms.[6]

James Cone is, actually, bringing into a modern context an insight first articulated by James Weldon Johnson in his study of the Negro spirituals:

> The Negro took as his basic material just his native African rhythms and the King James version of the Bible and out of them created the Spirituals.... In the Spirituals the Negro did express his religious hopes and fears, his faith and his doubts. In them he also expressed his theological and ethical views, and sounded his exhortations and warnings.... In a large proportion of the songs the Negro passed over the strict limits of religion and covered nearly the whole range of group experiences — the notable omission being sex.[7]

From the work we have done here, it should be easy to see that Johnson was prescient in allowing that the African rhythms were more than incidental. In the rhythms are the scholarly insights that Cone seems defensive about, and the rhythms are the foundations for the theological and ethical views, the warnings and the exhortations that Johnson recognizes. Stripped of all but the ability to express the most complex emotions in a pure sound, enslaved Africans reached across the barriers of language, culture, and circumstance to forge links to one another, in the midnight of the Middle Passage, with comforting sound. There was nothing else; nothing else was needed.

This, then, is the argument for how this study employs black sacred song as the foundation for African American theological endeavors: the songs take us back to the shores and ships of our history; the songs haunt the stories of enslavement, tragedy, and transcendence. Observers and participants provide a consensus: the sacred music of the enslaved Africans was as pervasive as the drum dancing of the cultures from whence they were snatched.

The abductive act of enslavement ruptured the cosmos of the Africans. Robert Farris Thompson details the rich symbolism of the "Kongo cosmogram" and supplies another layer of meaning to the form of resistance that was acted out, sung about, and remembered throughout African American history. As we have learned from *The Four Moments of the Sun:* we, through our initiations, follow the sun because we ourselves are second suns.[8]

Human beings are born and re-create the journey of the sun: the ultimate goal being to join the ancestors and become one with them in the land of the living (known) dead. If the human being is taken away from the land, then when death occurs, there will be no place of rest; no communion with the ancestors will be possible. Further, since the ancestors are actively involved in the social well-being of the community, being cut off from the ground wherein the ancestors dwell means that the adult human being cannot receive solace, support, or guidance from the ancestors. *Alienation* became radically and unalterably true with the introduction of European slavery to the west coast of Africa. The (human) sun could not complete its journey. The full meaning of life was lost. The circle was destroyed. The stability of the cosmos was undone. It was no longer possible to "stand upon the cross and swear both on God and the ancestors."

Separated from the home*land* by water, the enslaved African could no longer become an ancestor who could work on behalf of the family, of the clan. The desperation to return and the loss of meaning to one's life are themes still present in the religious music of African Americans and in the poetry, prose, and fiction derived from these songs. The songs known traditionally as "Negro spirituals" began on the decks of the ships and on the water. These songs, handed down in time, have been repositories of much more than musical patterns; strategies of survival and encoded documents of history and theology and sociology can all be found in the spirituals. Modern artists such as Richard Wright, Zora Hurston, James Baldwin, and Toni Morrison (to name only some of the more prominent descendants of the singer-prophets) continue the tradition, using the same aesthetic principles that can be discovered in the spirituals, and utilizing these artistic principles for the same reasons: to lead their companions on the dreadful journey out of the wilderness and into homeland.

Close study of these primary texts of African American theology counters a popular impression that the Christianity proselytized upon the enslaved Africans was a tool of the enslavers, used to render the enslaved into docile, submissive *creatures* who were eventually addicted to a religion that bound them internally to a vengeful God who demanded obedience and passivity in the face of the degradation inflicted upon them. African Americans did not leap into a chariot of faith that promised otherworldly redemption in exchange for *this*-worldly dehumanization. Any view that starts with such myopia rests its case on a presumption that the enslaved Africans were naive and unsuspecting objects of manipulation and coercion and of an emotional seduction aimed at human beings who, it is further assumed, were already disposed to primitive religious superstitions, to nonreflective rituals and practices, and to animistic cosmologies.

The evidence that emerges from within the African American religious tradition suggests that preachers, exhorters, prophets, visionaries, and bards knew that the world in which they found themselves was more than "cold and friendless" — it was complex, forbidding, hostile, and threatening to the well-being of mind, soul, and body. Such a world demanded equally complex reactions and strategies for survival. Why did the black and unknown bards *sing* their race to Christ? Because they were naturally gifted with artistic talents? Because theirs was a child-like constitution and self-awareness? Because they were primitive peoples and had, therefore, only primitive (precivilized) tools of survival at their disposal?

Arguments for the complexity of African American culture from its beginnings and from "behind the veil" can be found in the earliest literature dealing with the modern trans-Atlantic African slavery. The most complex voice from the early "slave narratives" belongs to Olaudah Equiano (or Gustavus Vassa). When Equiano remembers his origins, he claims for his people a level of sophistication that seldom receives adequate attention. To repeat a passage cited earlier: "Every great event, such as a triumphant return from battle, or other cause of public rejoicing is celebrated in public dances, which are accompanied with songs and music suited to the occasion."[9]

Slavery attempted to erase the rituals of *triumph*, but slavery could not destroy the motive or the method of commemoration — the ritual. Frederick Douglass provides a reflection on the music and the rituals of commemoration; that reflection not only will inform W. E. B. Du Bois in *The Souls of Black Folk*, but serves as an early example of the transformation of African culture through the necessities of African American slave life. Douglass responds to Equiano, showing how the aesthetic choices are maintained:

> The slaves selected to go to the Great House Farm, for the monthly allowance for themselves and their fellow-slaves, were peculiarly enthusiastic. While on their way, they would make the dense old woods, for miles around, reverberate with their wild songs, revealing at once the highest joy and the deepest sadness. They would compose as they went along, consulting neither time nor tune. The thought that came up, came out — if not in the word, in the sound; — and as frequently in the one as in the other.[10]

From triumphant returns from battle to the collection of the monthly allowance: the universe of concerns has been reduced in scale. But the remnant in diaspora remembers the forms of culture (the "African survivals"), and these forms are maintained with recognizable continuity.

In the earlier work, Equiano instructs an audience completely ignorant of the culture that produced him. In offering his memories of his home, he establishes a moral challenge to his readers. *This* African was no pagan in need of the ameliorating hand of civilization. The more Equiano learned while among his captors, the more he valued his origins. He challenges the assumptions of his audience, while ostensibly offering an "interesting" narrative, not a blatant polemic or an apology.

While Douglass is engaged in a passionate argument against slavery, his method is the same as that utilized by Equiano fifty years before: take an observable communal act and subvert the popular understanding held by the reading audience. Douglass understands very well the tendency for his audience to define the singing in its least complex understanding. An eloquent voice from within and without the circle of slave culture, Douglass demands that the multiple realities of slave music (and *life* and *thought*) be recognized:

> To those songs I trace my first glimmering conception of the dehumanizing character of slavery. I can never get rid of that conception. Those songs still follow me, to deepen my hatred of slavery, and quicken my sympathies for my brethren in bonds. . . . I have often been utterly astonished, since I came to the north, to find persons who could speak of the singing, among slaves, as evidence of their contentment and happiness. It is impossible to conceive of a greater mistake. Slaves sing when they are most unhappy. The songs of the slave represent the sorrows of his heart; and he is relieved by them, only as an aching heart is relieved by its tears.[11]

Within these thoughts, those of both Equiano and Douglass, can be found seeds of an African American aesthetic that informs and nourishes the production of art even today. Every event can be commemorated by art, as would be expected of the descendants of nations of "musicians, dancers and poets." Art is not an elitist undertaking, therefore. All members of the community can be looked to for creative responses to the occurrences of life. A work of art that can reveal simultaneously the "highest joy and the deepest sadness" must be carefully analyzed, for the meaning in the work will be highly contextual and dependent on the *intentionality* of the artist.[12] These remarks of Equiano and Douglass suggest multiple layers of meaning hidden behind the veil of the enthusiastic and often unsettling performances of African American music and religious rituals that were remarked upon by various observers and visitors to the South — many of whom understood that what they saw was merely a glimpse of a much larger world.[13]

The reduction in scale that has been noted does not imply an incompleteness. In fact the reduction is only *symbolic*. It can be strongly argued that the displaced Africans used the creative powers of their imaginations to create new limits of existence to counteract the constrictions and destructions of slavery. They did not "sing a race from wood and stone to Christ," as much as they sang themselves from small groups of individuals into a *people*, from the brink of collective psychic collapse to a place where systems of psychological health could be generated and sustained. John Blassingame focuses on this in *The Slave Community:*

> In religion, a slave exercised his own independence of conscience. Convinced that God watched over him, the slave bore his earthly afflictions in order to earn a heavenly reward.... Religious faith gave an ultimate purpose to his life, a sense of communal fellowship and personal worth, and reduced suffering from fear and anxiety. In short, religion helped him to preserve his mental health. Trust in God was conducive to psychic health insofar as it excluded all anxiety-producing preoccupations by the recognition of a loving Providence.[14]

In order to demonstrate that the reduction of the universe of African American aesthetic discourse does not imply any procrustean trimming, it would be profitable to introduce, at this point in the discussion, several additional elements of Thompson's "aesthetic of the cool." While Thompson's study of African and African American art focuses mainly on the visual and dynamic arts, his insights can also be appropriated easily into a discussion of philosophy, theology, and literature.

In *Flash of the Spirit*, Thompson begins his explanation of *minkisi* (the plural of *nkisi*) with this description given by Nsemi Isaki:

> [*Nkisi*] is the name of the thing we use to help a person when that person is sick and from which we obtain health.... It is also called *nkisi* because there is one to protect the human soul and guard it against illness for whoever is sick and wishes to be healed. An *nkisi* is also a chosen companion, in whom all people find confidence. It is a hid-

ing place for people's souls, to keep and compose in order
to preserve life.[15]

An *nkisi,* obviously, becomes the tool of the therapeutic rituals invoked by the description found in the words of John
Blassingame. Religious faith gave ultimate meaning to a slave's
life. Religious practice and ritual became "a hiding place," a protection for the soul. "There is a balm in Gilead, to heal the
sin-sick soul. There is a balm in Gilead, to make the wounded
whole." The balm discovered in this spiritual journey found expression in the songs of faith. The songs become active agents in
causing the effect they describe. Into the songs the believers can
pour their souls, creating the healing community (if we were to
follow the path that Blassingame suggests).

Thompson offers his own elaboration to the definition he
obtains from Nsemi Isaki:

> *Minkisi* containers are various: leaves, shells, packets, sa-
> chets, bags, ceramic vessels, wooden images, statuettes,
> cloth bundles, among other objects. Each *nkisi* contains
> medicines (*bilongo*) and a soul (*mooyo*), combined to give
> it life and power. The medicines themselves are spirit-
> embodying and spirit-directing.[16]

We may add to the list of *minkisi* containers the sacred objects
often named in African and African American spirituals and
gospel songs — and eventually, we must add the songs themselves
to the list. "I got *shoes* (*robe, crown, wings, harp*)." "We are climbing Jacob's *ladder.*" The *rock* in a weary land. The *Jordan River*
(in its many aspects, but especially when it "chills the body and
not the soul"). The *chariot* of Elijah. The *wheels within wheels*
of Ezekiel's vision. The holy *number* and the *Book of the Seven
Seals* of John the Revelator. The *ram-lamb-sheep horns* of Joshua's
noisy band. The *lions' den* temporarily inhabited by Daniel (along
with all the other imprisoning spaces of scripture).

Each of these containers of medicines and soul (and many,
many more) works wonders on the believers who sing and listen
and sway to the telling of the stories. The songs become medici-

nal because the singers attest that they will *sing, shout,* and never
grow weary; that they don't feel no ways tired while they sing
of their deliverance. The act of singing and praying is therapeutic. "A man went down to the River; he went down there for to
pray, . . . and his soul got happy and he stayed all day." "I've got
to live the life I sing about in my song."

Further into his discussion of *minkisi,* Thompson directs his
readers' attention to the symbolic/metaphorical function of several of the *minkisi:* to represent the world in miniature ("the
cosmos miniaturized") by combining aspects of the world designed by the Kongo cosmogram.[17] "Representing the world in
miniature" is exactly the function of the songs of the spirituals
tradition. As would be true of the sacramental objects of most
world religions, the *minkisi* serve as "mediating objects," meaning
that the object in hand directs the bearer to consider the larger
universe of faith inhabited by creatures of myth; divine agents;
the spirits of the dead; and the human beings who presently walk
the earth:

> Feathers in Kongo connote ceaseless growth as well as
> plenitude. So if the earth within the charm affirms the
> presence of a spirit from the dead — from the under-
> world — feathers capping the charm suggest connection
> with the upper half of the Kongo cosmogram which rep-
> resents the world of the living, and the empyrean habitat
> of God.[18]

Equiano, Douglass, and Du Bois all understood the songs to
contain a "world of meaning," that they are texts to be unlocked
and studied, are sources of confirmation and nourishment and
understanding. Whether the songs create and constitute a "nation" of singers and dancers and poets, or serve as the anthems
and companions of a band of slaves moving toward a plantation
"big house" (or toward the Jordan River of freedom, the Ohio),
the music *functions* similarly. The elements of the world are
bound together and become *sources* of power within the songs.
The songs, embodying power, direct the activities of the singers
and the listeners.

In *Army Life in a Black Regiment,* Thomas Wentworth Higginson provides some of the clearest examples of artistic *appropriation,* of the management of the spiritual world through the creation of dynamic *minkisi,* and examples of the development of new theological perspectives which constitute the beginnings of African and African American spirituality. At the end of the chapter "Negro Spirituals," Higginson records what was, for him, a minor and amusing anecdote of how his "dusky troops" could misappropriate the English language in their attempts to express their exhilaration in being allowed to fight in the Union Army during the Civil War. Given the aesthetic emerging here, an element of which is the presumption that the African and African American community had a desperate historical need to control the language it used and the language by which it was defined, Higginson's remarks about his troops (in *Army Life* and elsewhere) can be seen to possess multiple layers of significance and meaning, some of which contradict Higginson's culturally predictable interpretations.

If one does not attribute a love of words or a highly developed linguistic facility to the poets who "sang their race to Christ," then the poetic result could be described as a *felix culpa* (a fortuitous accident).[19] If, however, a poetic impulse is actively shaping the raw material according to traditional principles of artistic creation (principles easily borne across the Atlantic during the centuries of the Middle Passage), then the result might be judged in remarkably different terms. Colonel Higginson writes:

> As they learned all their songs by ear, they often strayed into wholly new versions, which sometimes became popular, and entirely banished the others. This was amusingly the case, for instance, with one phrase in the popular campsong of "Marching Along," which was entirely new to them until our quartermaster taught it to them, at my request. The words, "gird on the armor," were to them a stumbling block, and no wonder, until some ingenious ear substituted, "Guide on de army," which was at once accepted, and became universal.

"We'll guide on de army, and be marching along" is now the established version on the Sea Islands.[20]

The changed lyric not only reflects the real role of the African and African American soldier in the Civil War but also serves as a summary of many of Higginson's comments on the role of the black soldier, found elsewhere in his writings. These soldiers and their families did in fact become the guides and teachers of Higginson and his fellow officers; their bravery, constancy, decorum, and passion for achieving their own undisputed liberty at first shamed the unbelieving and resistant North while they quickened the hearts of other Africans and African Americans, slave and free.

Higginson more than once refers to the assessment that the black troops were superior in matters of courtesy; in the learning of military discipline; in the mastering of technology; in civilized behavior; in their lacking a sense of "refined and ingenious evil." In a moment fresh with simplicity and directness, Higginson makes a statement which serves as a model of his deep respect and which at the same time permits the speculation that the African and African American troops were self-consciously reaffirming what was for them a holy call to become the children of Moses marching into a/the Promised Land:

> As well might he who had been wandering for years upon the desert, with a Bedouin escort, discuss the courage of the men whose tents have been his shelter and whose spears his guard. We, their officers, did not go there to teach lessons but to receive them. There were more than a hundred men in the ranks who had voluntarily met more dangers in their escape from slavery than any of my young captains had incurred in all their lives.[21]

In *The Sable Arm*, Dudley Taylor Cornish provides an account of a scene so closely similar to that provided by Higginson as to lead one to wonder if there are not heretofore unremarked ritual spaces to be found in the accounts of African and African American presence in the wars of America. (What is even more remarkable is that the song being "spontaneously" appropriated is a variation on the song recorded by Higginson — and appropriated for much the same effect as described in *Army Life*.) Cornish is writing about the preparations for an assault planned for July 30, 1864, in northern Virginia. The action would have involved over four thousand African and African American soldiers, who had been assigned to lead the assault:

> The men reacted curiously to the news that they would lead. As Colonel Thomas put it, "the news put them too full for ordinary utterance." They sat silent in little circles in their company streets until a single deep voice began to sing, rather tentatively at first and then over and over with a hardening conviction: "We-e looks li-ike me-en a-a-marchin' on, we looks li-ike men-er-war." Then the singer's circle took up the shout and it rapidly spread through the encampment until "a thousand voices were upraised...." And the voices of a thousand Negro soldiers, making their own harmony, lifting the words up into the night sky like some great shapeless battle flag: "We looks like men a-marching on, we looks like men er war." "Until we fought the battle of the crater," Colonel Thomas remembered, "they sang this every night to the exclusion of all other songs."[22]

These soldiers were preparing themselves through a ritual that was obviously religious. Many of the elements of the construction of the spirituals are detailed in this scene: call-and-response; repetition; identification with great heroes; use of the dance circle; building a trance state for the purpose of support and exhortation and for the ritual of spirit-possession. This is not a matter of instinct and spontaneous invention. As Equiano pointed out, decades earlier, warriors preparing for battle sang the proper songs. These African and African American soldiers took the role of leading the army to be of high significance. Perhaps not knowing the specific songs sung by their African ancestors, they nevertheless knew that *singing* was essential; so they created an *nkisi*. When Joshua "fit the battle of Jericho," he had the power of music and dance and shouting to effect the victory. "I'm singing with a sword in my hand." "We looks like men of war."

A Voice Crying Out

The black Union soldiers and their families who attended them in the army camps were responsible for many of the songs we know today as Negro spirituals. More pertinently, they and their families were examples of how a *performance theology* might be understood to be truly African and African American, and Catholic. The soldiers sang themselves into existence as heroes, as guides, as "soldiers of the cross." The songs they used for prayer were instruments of building a community of support (a circle of power), and the songs and prayers of the community so gathered had a specific purpose: the liberation of those who sang and danced and prayed, and the liberation of countless others who were voiceless, constrained or shackled by the oppression of slavery.

In the previous chapter, in remarks dealing with African and African American ecstasy, it was suggested that further reflections should be undertaken into the ways that Africans and African Americans made use of "intermediary elements" in order to achieve mystical union with the power of the divine. The descriptions Colonel Thomas Wentworth Higginson offers of the black Union troops in prayer should provide us with important insights into how the "black and unknown bards" of African and African American Christianity sang themselves "from wood and stone to Christ," how the composers of the spirituals learned to "fly without ever leaving the ground," to appropriate a phrase from Toni Morrison.[23] Higginson's descriptions of the "ring shouts" entered into by the troops under his command are the clearest renderings we have from the nineteenth-century sociologists who did so much to preserve records of African and African American rituals. Because these descriptions mirror the dances of the drum circle so remarkably well, Higginson's remarks will be studied at some length.

As he begins his first description of a shout, Higginson provides some highly evocative details surrounding the creation of a "sacred space" for the rituals. Palm-leaf "booths" are constructed, inside of which fires burn. Around these fires, soldiers are crammed together tightly, and the men are "singing at the top of their voices, in one of their quaint, monotonous, endless, negro-Methodist chants, with obscure syllables recurring constantly, with slight variations interwoven, all accompanied with a regular drumming of the feet and clapping of the hands, like castanets."[24] Higginson then presents a picture of the emergence of an ecstatic ritual that prefigures the observations (and directly influences the interpretations) of all of the modern scholars who study this phenomenon:

> [I]nside and outside the enclosure men begin to quiver and dance, others join, a circle forms, winding monotonously round some one in the centre; some "heel and toe" tumultuously, others merely tremble and stagger on, others stoop and rise, others whirl, others caper sideways, all keep steadily circling like dervishes; spectators applaud special strokes of skill.[25]

These — and similar — scenes take place constantly during nights in camp. The soldiers seem strengthened, confirmed, rejuvenated, Higginson notes. He also presents a picture of the inclusiveness of these rituals that may, ironically, speak far better than he realized about the black Union soldiers' ability to understand exactly what their divinely inspired mission was:

> [M]y approach only enlivens the scene; the circle enlarges, louder grows the singing, rousing shouts of encouragement come in, half bacchanalian, half devout, "Wake 'em, brudder!" "Stan' up to 'em, brudder!" — and still the ceaseless drumming and clapping, in perfect cadence, goes steadily on. Suddenly there comes a sort of *snap*, and the spell breaks, amid general sighing and laughter. And this not rarely and occasionally, but night after night, while in other

parts of the camp the soberest prayers and exhortations are proceeding sedately.[26]

The ritual itself should interest us most, at this time. The "snap" observed by Higginson could just as easily be described as the moment when ecstasy, having been achieved by members of the group, cannot be physically sustained any longer. Or we might speculate that the ritual is completed only when the rhythms and the chanting have compelled the colonel to join the circle, and to be renamed and blessed by the community in his new identity as "brother." However we understand or interpret the ritual, it should be obvious that the term "bacchanalian" is not appropriate.

The men of the circle are maintaining an observance of sacred rituals that seem to have sustained the black Union soldiers everywhere they assembled. The holy dance of the drum circle continues to call down the power of God upon and within the practitioners. The power so received provides the ability to change reality, beginning with the process of giving things (and persons) new names, and therefore new functions within the community. Many an observer may have looked upon the black Union soldiers as experiments or as exotic representatives of primitive cultures, but the soldiers saw themselves as "guides of the army," soldiers of God, mighty men of war. They saw themselves as the mighty army of the heavenly host, waging war with the forces of Satan.

We must understand that the voices of the African and African American singers captured the imaginations of their listeners for a very good reason. The singing of Africans and African Americans (both enslaved and nominally free) was described almost rotely as "weird," "plaintive," "haunting," "of a minor key," "melancholy," "wailing," and, of course, "filled with sorrow." The power of the singing affected the hearers in a multiplicity of ways. I make the claim that the singers knew of their effect, and that effect was to change the reality of singer and listener alike, based on this understanding of the intentionality of the artist.

In order to establish the argument for such "prophetic utterance," we need to remember the discussion on *àshe* (the Yoruba term meaning "the power to make things happen"). We need to remember, also, that biblical utterance and the language often derived from such utterance are thought of as qualitatively different from other forms of rhetoric. In his magisterial study of the Bible and literature, Northrup Frye calls such utterance *kerygmatic* language:

> [The linguistic idiom of the Bible] is really a fourth form of expression, for which I adopt the now well-established term *kerygma,* proclamation. . . . *Kerygma* is a mode of rhetoric, though it is rhetoric of a special kind. . . . It is the vehicle of what is traditionally called revelation. . . . The Bible is far too deeply rooted in all the resources of language for any simplistic approach to its language to be adequate. . . . [M]yth is the linguistic vehicle of *kerygma.*[27]

The meaning of *kerygma* can be amplified to include "words imbued with power." As part of the definitions of *kerygma,* we must absorb the following: "Because there exists an inner unity between the words in Sacred Scripture and the events to which they point and which they proclaim, the language of the kerygma about God's salvific acts of power in and through Jesus Christ is a veritable epiphany or divine self-expression."[28]

The religious figures who were responsible for the composition and continuance of the body of sacred song known as the Negro spirituals were part of a religious tradition that demanded that each practitioner undergo extensive physical practices which would induce mystical experiences, by which they would become vessels of the divine, transmitters of revelations, and human beings transformed by their possession by the Holy Spirit. Whatever words or sounds they uttered were *proclaimed* for the conversion of all who would hear them. The songs they composed in such states of ecstasy and prophecy were created to be proclamations and testimonies of revelations given to the singers on behalf of the community. The drum dances of western African and African cultures were transformed into "shouts" and "camp meetings," whereby the congregants called down the divine into their midst, with an important variation stemming from their appropriation of Christian imagery and mythologies.

The ecstatic state took the devotee to heaven, where the vision was bestowed, and the chosen one was given the mission of returning to the world in order to proclaim what was seen and heard. The physical manifestation of spirit-possession served, therefore, an added function: it was proof of "transportation." The "getting of the Holy Spirit" authenticated the message that would be proclaimed when the receptor had ended the mystical link. When all the participants were "slain in the spirit," then what had formed was a "sanctified" community (or "church") which had the obligation of living the life they sang about in their song. What is true in Sanctified, Pentecostal, and Spiritualist churches today was just as true of the African and African American participants in the Methodist and Baptist revivals that burned up the English-speaking United States and West Indies from the early 1700s to the early 1900s.[29]

In this long-lived climate of religious fervor, Africans and African Americans were centrally involved in both the preaching and the hearing of the word. Moreover, the word of God was alive everywhere in America. The special vitality of this word, bringing a message of liberation, was seized upon by Africans and African Americans with a special twist. One of the methods of liberation was the realization that Jesus gave the power (the sending of the Holy Spirit) to *do* what he did: speak with authority. Africans and African Americans, therefore, had special reasons to believe that the truth would set them free — even (as was the case of Frederick Douglass and others) when the truth was kept from them, changed, diluted, or perverted.

They took upon themselves the role of manipulators, renewers, and restorers of the word of God. The role of "prophets of justice and righteousness," disciples of truth, became a primary task, a proof of their witness. They sought conversion, in order to receive their anointing (being slain in the Spirit), so that they could return from heaven with a message of life and liberty for all the captives. Having kept faith with their African and African American origins, they became not only *doers* of the word but also *dancers of their revelations*. Having achieved an inner unity between received word and human receptor, they became — at least for the time of their prophesying, of their giving witness — *embodiments* of the word. They made of themselves the heroes of the Bible come back to the earth, their own ancestors present once more for the health and balance of the people; and they became carriers of the power to make things happen: vessels of grace.

In my mind this helps to explain the preponderance of heroic figures in the spirituals and the heavy reliance on a "heavenly point of view" employed in the songs. The prophets and warriors of the Old Testament are more than role models: they are the divinely graced figures who are called down for possession by the congregants. The songs employ a perspective of drama that is often unnoticed. The singers assume certain "voices" which indicate just who is controlling the song, the dance, the ritual. Old folks exhort the "children." Prophets direct the sacred action ("Swing low, sweet chariot"; "Oh, Peter, go ring them bells"). Spirit-possession even allows one to take on the voice of God, occasionally ("Go down, Moses"). Of all the role models mentioned in the spirituals, however, there is one group that dominates. From the moment that the singers realize that all of God's children have wings and harps as well as shoes, there is a determination to "join the heavenly band" (or "choir").

The self-adoption, not only into the chosen people of God ("see that band all dressed in red / must be the band that Moses led"), but into a special cadre of servants — the messengers of the judgment of God (the angels) — can be traced throughout the spirituals. It is this identification with angels that captures the attention of Colonel Higginson, and which provides him with striking examples of how the black Union soldiers prepared themselves to wage a holy war for freedom. Central to this discussion of how African and African American spiritual geniuses laid the groundwork for the enduring rock that is the black church are the theological and cultural implications of Africans and African Americans singing themselves into the

roles of the physical manifestations of the words of God —
into the roles of messengers, guides, and warriors of holiness.
Higginson heard these voices crying in the wilderness of South
Carolina military camps and was forever affected by the sounds
and dances of the soldiers. We, with the benefit of a slightly
better perspective, can remember that the voices crying in the
wilderness had something to say:

> In the wilderness prepare the way of the Lord,
>   make straight in the desert a highway for our God.
> Every valley shall be lifted up,
>   and every mountain and hill be made low;
> the uneven ground shall become level,
>   and the rough places a plain.
> Then the glory of the Lord shall be revealed,
>   and all people shall see it together,
>   for the mouth of the Lord has spoken. (Isa. 40:3–5)

Higginson also offered the lyrics to some of the songs used
for trance-inducement, and these lyrics established a theology of
prophetic witness that became the foundation for African and
African American spirituality as it is practiced still. The black
and unknown bards, once again, seem to have known exactly
what their singing would accomplish: they would make of themselves the mouth of the Lord. After all, they proclaimed, "We
are climbing Jacob's ladder."

Second Meditation

Climbing Jacob's Ladder

The devastation wreaked on the victims of the Middle Passage was never absolute, never final, never complete. Some survived; some resisted; some eventually restored to themselves a measure of the humanity that had been violently and perversely torn from their consciousness. No mistake should ever be made regarding an assessment of the culpability and the consequences of the transatlantic trade in human beings. Millions and millions of lives were lost; millions more would wish for death, once they found out what the life of enslavement would bring them. Centuries of systematic torture, manipulation, abuse, and domination of human beings by other human beings have brought into the world a pattern of psychosis and destructive behaviors that has infected cultures and peoples everywhere.

Perhaps the greatest problem with understanding the fact of this tragic period of human history lies within the *ability* to understand. The fierce resistance to accepting the fact that some human beings determined the shape and scope of the transatlantic slave trade brings us to the great stumbling block connected with the enslavement of Africans from the late 1400s to the late 1800s. The enslavers knew what they were doing and continued the practice of the enslavement of human beings because they wanted to. In some ways, at least in my mind at this stage of my life, the foundation of modernist thought seems to have arrived as a response to this implacable reality.

If a practice as heinous as the transatlantic slave trade could endure for four centuries, then those who controlled and bene-fited from the practice must have felt that the reward outweighed

the spiritual and psychological cost even to themselves. Let us
not fall into the modern fallacy: there are consequences to one's
behavior. We, all of us, are responsible for our own actions and
must accept the reckoning for our deeds. To counter that human
beings are adrift from all harbors of meaning, that each individual is alienated and stands outside the possibility of absolute
truth and human community, is to advance an argument of great
attraction, especially for those who would resist turning a relentless gaze upon their own past. When that task becomes too
expensive to undertake, it is altogether understandable if many
(even most) would argue that the past is not usable, that it
cannot be trusted, and that all efforts to make sense of one's actions are — however heroic the effort — ultimately a tragic leap
of faith.

History has become the two-edged sword of cultural and ethnic identity for all Americans. *Race* and *color* and, to a growing
extent, even *ethnicity* are more often now admitted to be what
they always were: political constructs whose vitality depends on
an agreement as to what the terms mean and what significance
they have in the public discourse. Countless futile arguments
over what it means to be "black" or "white" and over the math-
ematical permutations on determining "Hispanic" identities only
prove this assertion. "Who defines the terms by which we live?"
should be a mantra for the times in which we live. The names
by which we are known are not as important as the names to
which we answer, folk wisdom tells us. But, then, that same folk
wisdom has told us, from the time of our infancy: "Sticks and
stones may break my bones, but words will never hurt me." In
the multiple cultures that are called "American," nothing was
ever less true than that childhood rhyme. *Words* can be criminal; can invoke mistrust, violence, riots; can lead to the denial of
medical benefits, the withholding of security in employment and
housing. Words (or the withholding of them) can lead to death.

The struggle over the true names of things is an issue of essential importance to every creature that lives, to every thing that
has an existence. In the Christian faith-tradition the true name
of things (the distribution of nouns, as it were) begins with the

opening verses of Genesis and ends with the visions of John the Divine in the writings on the Apocalypse. And from the opening pages of Genesis, we know that "words," just as surely as the weapon used by Cain, can kill the other.

Violence is the ultimate resource used for making definitions adhere to the "object" in question. Violence must be constantly renewed in order to make the definitions endure, until such time as the acceptance of the proper name has been internalized by all those affected. Racism follows this pattern with an inevitability that is complete. All systems of tyranny and oppression participate in this dynamic, however. The violence of terrorism, either state-sponsored (war) or more locally generated (guerrilla or vigilante activities), has little or no trust in persuasion, unless it is in the service of physical domination.

The claim of covenant in African American theology takes on an added significance when we regard it as a response to the degradations of enslavement. The dynamic of self-naming and the reliance on appropriating the great heroes of liberation from the Bible begin to make more sense when we reflect on how devastating it is to be called *whore*, and *nigger*, and *bastard*, and *bitch*, and *dog*, and *animal*, and *slave*. Such naming eventually acquired legal sanction. "Who defines the terms by which we live" must be sounded with the same moans that invest "Sometimes I feel like a motherless child."

It is in this context that we might absorb the full meaning of Higginson's response to one of the campfire songs popular with the soldiers under his command. His comments "speak far better than [he] knew," dealing as they do with mysticism and hero-appropriation. The remainder of this study will be fed by the authority of the singing and praying of these biblical heroes come back to life. Only by assuming an evangelical mission, undertaking a life of prophetic utterance, can the African Americans who call themselves church create a community which will love mercy, do justice, and walk humbly with the Lord (Mic. 6:8). The sly reading of the story of Jacob is filled with humor, confidence, and faith; without these qualities righteousness and justice cannot be achieved. In order to restore the balance that may have been undone by selfishness and individualism, the African dancers and singers had to hold up the disordered behavior to the eyes of the community and demand that the proper rituals be undertaken for the healing of all affected. The agonistic struggle with the forces of darkness and with the lower nature of humanity is a theme present everywhere in ascetic writings. To find the same agonistic endeavor in a Civil War army camp is a revelation:

> The next is one of the wildest and most striking of the whole series: there is a mystical effect and a passionate striving throughout the whole. The Scriptural struggle between Jacob and the angel, which is only dimly expressed in the words, seems all uttered in the music. I think it impressed my imagination more powerfully than any other of these songs.

XIX. Wrestling Jacob

O wrestlin' Jacob, Jacob, day's a-breakin';
  I will not let thee go!
O wrestlin' Jacob, Jacob, day's a-breakin';
  He will not let me go!
O, I hold my brudder wid a tremblin' hand;
  I would not let him go!
I hold my sister wid a tremblin' hand;
  I would not let her go!
O, Jacob do hang from a tremblin' limb;
  He would not let him go![1]

It is a ring shout; it is a method of trance-inducement. The song calls forth the divine through the act of self-naming and by the act of restoring a right relationship (balance) in the community. The singers (*plural* because the rhetorical "I" reinforces the autonomy of each member of the circle: equality is possible only among a community of similarly empowered persons) have done the work of theologians, taking the story and making an application that is particular to their circumstances. By focusing on one of the most disreputable of God's favored patriarchs, the singers perform an act of deconstruction of the text that would make the most sophisticated postmodernist critic envious. Before the story of Jacob wrestling till the break of day can be studied, we need to remember how Jacob came to be on the Plain of Peniel in the first place.

The Story of Jacob

Isaac was the son of Abraham and Sarah, the son that Abraham nearly sacrificed to Yahweh as proof of his faithfulness to his newly found God-above-all-other-gods. Isaac married his kinswoman Rebecca. Praying to the God of Abraham (and Sarah, since she too had much to do with the inheritance of faith) on behalf of his wife's barrenness, Isaac found himself to be the expectant parent of twins. Isaac and Rebecca's sons were Esau and Jacob.

At the birth of the twins, Esau was delivered first, but even in their mother's womb the twins struggled for domination, with Jacob emerging grasping his brother's ankle. The prophecy announcing their birth declared that the sons would divide two peoples and that the elder would serve the younger. Esau was a hunter, while Jacob was a quiet man, dwelling in tents. Isaac favored Esau, and Rebecca favored Jacob. Both seemed oblivious of the implications of the prophecy surrounding their children.

During a fit of hunger Esau was persuaded — coerced — to sell his "birthright" (his status as the first-born) for a meal that Jacob had conveniently waiting for him upon his return from a hunting expedition. The promised inheritance given to the family of Abraham was thus traded in that generation for dinner.

But the inheritance of the covenant was always in contradiction to the laws of inheritance prevailing in those times and places. The eldest traditionally inherited all the property of the parent. In the adventure story that is biblical history, the second-born son wins the favor of the parent (God figure) and gets the best of the property — this is true from Cain to the "prodigal son" of the Gospel of Luke. And usually the second-born has less to recommend him to the good will of the reader of the story. Liars, murderers, thieves, men given over to passionate excesses — these "favored" children seem more like spoiled brats. The truths of redemption are often hard to accept.

There is an inevitability to the behavior of Esau. After all, the "elder will serve the younger" had been recited around him from his conception. "Thus Esau despised his birthright" (Gen. 25:34). Toward what he thought was the end of his life, Isaac, we are told, grew blind and feeble. Wishing to impart his blessing (the legal sanction bestowing the right of inheritance upon the eldest son) upon Esau, he summoned his son and asked of him a meal of the wild game that Esau hunted. Perhaps this version of Oedipal hubris needs to be studied as closely as the version employed by Freud. The blindness of Isaac seems a result of his obsession with forgetting the power of the prophecies of Yahweh. By his determination to give Esau the advantage, Isaac made himself blind to the inevitability of Yahweh's (and Rebecca's) designs for Jacob. Or perhaps Isaac merely had to perform his part in the ritual for the instruction of the observers of the sacred drama.

As soon as Esau departed in search of the game, Rebecca (whose sight and hearing were in no way diminished by age and who had heard of Isaac's request) summoned her favored son and effected an act of deception upon both Isaac and Esau. She prepared a meal that would satisfy Isaac's gustatory expectations. She would feed the delusions of a blind old man, and she would disguise Jacob in the hides and fur of wild animals, dousing him with the scent of the fields that he might prevail over his brother in their father's heart as he had contended with Esau in Rebecca's womb.

The deception worked, and when Esau arrived with the now-superfluous meal, only a secondary blessing remained for the speaking. Jacob had to flee for his life, for Esau and his children were consumed with rage. Rebecca advised Jacob to retrace his father's footsteps and journey to the east to meet with her brother Laban, to find a wife, and to settle among a distant people who were his own kin. One of Esau's sons overtook Jacob on this flight and stripped him of all his possessions. The threat of death and burial seems to be a part of this family quest for its inheritance. Soon after this abasement, Jacob came to rest at a holy hill (which he later named Bethel), and there Jacob dreamed a dream: "And he dreamed that there was a ladder set up on the earth, the top of it reaching heaven; and the angels of God were ascending and descending on it" (Gen. 28:12). The voice of God was with Jacob, and Jacob was forthright enough to bargain with God: if you are favorable to me, Jacob said, then I will worship you as my parents and grandparents did. In keeping with the divine disregard for human expectations that is found throughout these stories, Yahweh agrees to the conditional covenant.

Jacob went to live with his uncle Laban. There he worked as an extremely charismatic shepherd. Jacob contracted to work for seven years, as a bride-payment for the right to wed Rachel, Laban's younger daughter. On the wedding night Leah, the elder sister, was veiled and given to Jacob in an act of deception. No matter how much Jacob protested the deception, Laban was adamant that the elder should have precedence over the younger — obviously a concept Jacob would find unusual. Laban forced him to work for another seven years in order to receive Rachel. After more than twenty years of work, craftiness, blessings, increase and the manipulation of several women who were pawns in the sexual bartering connected with the conception of legal heirs, Jacob and his "possessions" (wives and children most decidedly counted in that reckoning) returned to meet Esau. Along the way, Jacob met angels once again, after his final encounter with Laban, concerning Rachel's forever-undiscovered theft of her father's household gods.

By taking away the very spiritual foundation of her family's worth and status, Rachel undermined her father's authority and brought her own inheritance for the benefit of her children. The gods were hidden within her clothes, and her deception was masked by her menstruation period. Nothing more secret or foreboding could have been claimed than this act of women's mystery rites. And thus Rachel endowed her children, Joseph and Benjamin. When Laban was unsuccessful in finding the purloined statues, he blessed Jacob, and the two households parted.

When Jacob met the angels after this familial parting, he called
the place the "camp of God" (Gen. 32:1).

The night before Jacob's intended meeting with his long-
estranged brother, he met with a stranger on the plain that Jacob
named "Peniel" — "the face of God," an apt name. The third encounter with the embodiment of God brought with it a message
for Jacob that would forever change him, and all of faith history. The message was physical and spiritual and aesthetic and
mythic: as should be true of all the best messages and the stories
wherein they are contained. When the "man" encountered Jacob,
they both wrestled until the break of day:

> When the man saw that he did not prevail against Jacob,
> he struck him on the hip socket; and Jacob's hip was put
> out of joint as he wrestled with him. Then he said, "Let
> me go, for the day is breaking." But Jacob said, "I will not
> let you go, unless you bless me."
>
> So he said to him, "What is your name?" And he said,
> "Jacob." Then the man said, "You shall no longer be called
> Jacob, but Israel [the one who strives with God], for you
> have striven with God and with humans, and have pre-
> vailed." Then Jacob asked him, "Please tell me your name."
> But he said, "Why is it that you ask my name?" And there
> he blessed him. (Gen. 32:25-30)

Jacob then went to his dreaded meeting with Esau; but instead
of the recriminations he deservedly expected, he was greeted
with tears of joy and embraces. The brothers then parted, each
to his own settlement, each to his own way of life; one to hunt
in the hills, one to dwell in tents and raise herds of cattle.

The story of brothers contending with brothers returns. The
exile and humiliation, the metaphoric death and enslavement of
the divinely favored, are part of every subsequent story of heroes,
from the children of Israel, to the children of David, to the
cousins John and Jesus.

If the story had not been chosen for song by the great African
American singer-prophets, we would be wise to appropriate it
now. But the story has been singled out for our consideration,

and no matter how the song is sung, Jacob is wrestled with; Jacob is the recipient of the messages; Jacob is caught, bone, sinew, and blood, in an embrace from which he can never flee.

When the old artists of black sacred song selected out of biblical mythology this identification with the angels on Jacob's ladder, and on the Plain of Peniel, they appropriated a role within the larger arena of American Christianity and within the space of the larger American society that explains, for better or for worse, many of the emphases — and the omissions — of African American culture that plague, intrigue, and exasperate many critics of African American culture to this day.

Within the myth of Jacob there is a primal conflict of brothers, struggling and contending with their respective roles in the single covenant with the divine; contending for the blessing — the naming, the identification of the *personhood* within the person (the aforementioned social reality of "who defines the terms by which we live"). In much of American society, people are who the group defines them to be, unfortunately, as often as they are who they determine themselves to be. The struggle is too often concerned with sloughing off the labels that mask identity and with resisting the stereotypes that suffocate rather than liberate.

The God who appears in the story of Jacob and his relatives is as much a problem as an answer. It is the prophetic intervention of this God that takes away Esau's social identity. It is the voice of this God that confirms Jacob (and his wife) in acts of treachery and familial betrayal. It is the physical manifestation of the power of this God that wrestles with Jacob and changes his name to Israel.

Jacob is an opportunist, a thief, a dissembler, and a coward. And those are his good qualities. He hedges his response to the covenant offered by the intervening God. He thereby dilutes the faith of his grandfather, Abraham, who was willing to kill his younger son, Isaac, believing in the ultimate benevolence of this new apparition of divine power, in spite of the inconsistency, cruelty, and contradictions in the commands of this God. Jacob wants the proof of the benevolence before he assents to the covenant.

The messengers of God, the angels of the ladder and the plain, do more than offer signs of worship and adoration (as is found in the visions of Daniel and Isaiah, for instance). They do more than confirm Yahweh's passionate disregard for the accepted inheritance laws of the prevailing society. These messengers are dream-figures representing violence, pain, and struggle. The "man" who appears from nowhere and wrestles with Jacob is an angel. That is clear. Jacob knew that much. That is why he "pushed his luck," as it were, and demanded to know the name of his adversary. By gaining his name, Jacob would have "won" the real wrestling match. The physical contending was a *sign*. At this point in biblical history, the storytellers do not allow the central characters any certitude surrounding this new god with strange demands (from circumcision to the absence of worship images, to primary obedience to a promise of some vague in-the-future dominion over the "nations").

Every other god, especially the familiar ones (the "household gods"), had forms, names, specific habitations. The "God of Abraham, of Jacob," could have seemed a small and petty entity, especially since all the looked-for benefits were generations down the line. If this god were to become the "God of Jacob," then Jacob wanted something concrete. Jacob had already proved appearances could be deceiving; and he had had the same lesson taught him by his father-in-law and his several wives. The point of the wrestling match was that Jacob needed to hear a name by which he could gain mastery over his adversary, and he did hear such a name: his own.

The wounding of Jacob is quite explicitly the beginning of his wisdom, because it is the radical act by which he is forced to a life of humility. The abasement that he prepares to offer Esau on the next day could be the remote psychic preparation of this dream encounter. His decision to return home and face the consequences of his act of usurpation was the beginning of the interior wrestling match. He struggled with himself, with his concept of divine favor, with the promptings of the divine within himself. He prevails. But he is not victorious. It is Jacob who limps away from the encounter. It is Jacob who tells his name. It is Jacob who, after a life of presumption and arrogance, hears his name given back, transformed by the trial he has endured.

In the first dream, that of the ladder, Jacob dreams with his eyes closed. The telling of the story of the second dream is constructed in such a way as to demand that we understand that Jacob was awake, that he faced up to his fears and his conflicted sense of God with his eyes wide open. The messenger of God comes to tell Jacob what he already knew. The God who demanded the faith of Jacob lived within him — not in a temple, not on a mountain, not in a rock. Jacob could believe that God would be with him with all the energy of his heart; but he would first have to accept the responsibility for all those actions he performed previously with a contingent faith in God. What Jacob prevailed over was his own self-delusions and his own arrogance. He would forever limp after his encounter with the God found in the solitary darkness.

Jacob would limp, in the eyes of his relatives, because he was seen groveling on the ground begging his brother's forgiveness. He would limp, in the eyes of the "people" (the people who carried the story within them), because he followed a law that, up until his own striving, made no sense and had no precedent. Part of Jacob was vanquished by the way he had made his dreams come true. In order to incorporate this spiritual striving into a language his people could understand — to show them a sign — he took upon himself the limp, the wounded hip, and the new name.

To be counted as one of the "children of Israel," any subsequent believer would have to assume some part of the identity of these figures of the myth. To believe in the divine consistency of purpose (as opposed to the shorter-sighted, human tendency to make sense of things: the problem confronting Job is the classic example of this); to have one's faith always directed to the future (instead of to the acquisition of wealth and property and a brood of children); to exercise the prodigal faith of Abraham; and to recognize with the heart of the *self* the indwelling of the power of God (even though this insight would place the believer in the position of being called an impractical fool, a dreamer, one "favored by women" — the descriptions of Abel, of Jacob, of Joseph, to name just a few) — these are components of the ancestral faith that are passed on, implicitly or explicitly, in every telling of the tale.[2]

We Are Climbing

The wounding of Jacob and the bearing of his true and deeper name seem the special province mapped out by African American spirituality as we have interpreted it here. We return, almost full circle, to the poem of James Weldon Johnson with which we opened this journey many pages ago:

> O black slave singers, gone, forgot, unfamed,
> You — you alone, of all the long, long line
> Of those who've sung untaught, unknown, unnamed,
> Have stretched out upward, seeking the divine.

Angels singing, stretching out and upward, to be sure; but doing even more than that, in that these messengers of incomparable courage and beauty and power come back with a text of deliverance. Salvation is not a private, selfish concern. The black slave singers knew that others were listening to, if not fully understanding, their sounds and gestures. The soldiers of the army camp under Colonel Higginson's command knew very well that he was listening and questioning and feeling overwhelmed by their expressions of militant Christianity. They enlarged the circle and called him "brother."

In the text of "Wrestling Jacob," we hear the singers identify both with the angel and with Jacob. It is from this doubled vision that much of the meditation presented here gains its motive. The singers exhort Jacob to continue the fight, and they are equally clear in presenting a narrative concerning Jacob. Soon, the song has performed an act of theological inclusion that should have been remarked upon by Higginson and that needs to be highlighted here: Jacob is both *brother* and *sister.* Women were an integral part of the army camp and of the religious observances of the African Americans housed in the camp. The names of the biblical heroes were assumed by those who functioned in the roles described in the songs. Harriet Tubman was known as (and called herself) "Moses." This is the same dynamic found in the Vodoun ceremonies of Haiti and the Candomblé rites of Brazil: the god (orisha, etc.) called down will possess the devotee, no matter the individual's gender. "Name follows function," in other words.

African American spirituality seems to find its uniqueness within the story of the wounding of Jacob and the bearing of his true and deeper name. And the role of *angel* is reserved to this spirituality, as it is to none of the other traditions prevalent within Christianity. From the earliest writings and records of African American Christianity, in fact, the prophetic authority of African American leaders is imbued with a visionary rhetoric that is so prevalent as to go mostly unremarked. Phillis Wheatley can speak with authority to George Washington and to aggressively heathenish undergraduates at Harvard College. Her authority stems from her acceptance of the "free grace of Methodism," of course, and her poetry is — no matter what else critics may say about her accomplishments — assured and utterly devoid of any sense of inferiority as she relates to the recipients of her poetic musings. So, too, with David Walker, in his *Appeal to the Colored Citizens of the World*. Walker's language and vision of the impending apocalypse that will be unleashed on the world if slavery continues are a warning and challenge to conversion. Walker is both Daniel and John the Revelator; he is utterly fearless even in taking on the contradictions and hypocrisy of the great secular saint of America's mythology, Thomas Jefferson. Most of the eighteenth-century writings of African Americans are as inspired as they are polemical and would be more easily seen as such if they were more often held up to the scrutiny of biblical prophetic language. The great orators and pamphleteers presented themselves as a moral force, girded and strengthened for the wrestling match that has lasted for the full night of cultural struggle that continues to inform the telling of the story of America.

The telling of the story makes a deeper, mythic sense when it becomes the story of the stolen inheritance; when it is told as a pattern of deceptions and counterdeceptions worked out within a family of wanderers; when it is the story of the word of judgment coming alive to contend and wrestle with the soul of the self-deceiving, manipulative "favored of God." It is not helpful to assume that the Africans who sang themselves from "wood and stone to Christ" were unaware of their audience. The singing they performed was medicinal, and not just for the singers.

When Thomas Jefferson made his midnight-of-the-soul confession in *Notes on the State of Virginia*, we can assure ourselves that it was his close interactions with the Africans of his environment and circumstance that caused him such honesty:

> And can the liberties of a nation be thought secure when we have removed their only firm basis, a conviction in the minds of the people that these liberties are of the gift of God? That they are not to be violated but with his wrath! Indeed I tremble for my country when I reflect that God is just: that his justice cannot sleep for ever: that considering numbers, nature and natural means only, a revolution of the wheel of fortune, an exchange of situation, is among possible events: that it may become probable by supernatural interference! The Almighty has no attribute which can take side with us in such a contest.[3]

And the prayerful wisdom found in the Second Inaugural Address of Abraham Lincoln would give support to the claim that he, too, had been long engaged in a midnight wrestling match with the true name of things, and that he could see the wounding of the soul of America in its obsession with the enslavement of some of its members.[4]

In the reading presented here of a biblical myth that has informed much of the rich tradition of African American spirituality, that is both reflective and engaged, that is both contemplative and prophetically active, the plain where Jacob wrestles with his angel is truly the place "where God strives." It is America. The founding ancestors of the spirituality presented here were denied the tents, flocks, tribes, riches, and possessions of either Jacob or Esau. They were not denied an awareness that their inheritance, their prophesied birthright, had been stolen from them. Choosing to reinforce their place in the telling of the story, they created a mystic space where truth is timeless, in the sense of being forever in the present.

Moses would live, contending with Pharaoh until the people of God were liberated (whether *Moses* be Harriet Tubman or Martin Luther King Jr.). Daniel would be cast into the furnace, be delivered and dream continually, until the people were no longer in exile (whether *Daniel* be David Walker or Fannie Lou Hamer). Joshua would call for nature to bow before the rightness of the claims of the chosen people of God until the artificial walls of cultural separation would fall into dust (whether *Joshua* be Frederick Douglass, W. E. B. Du Bois, or Marian Wright Edelman). And the angels would continue their journey between heaven and earth, bringing only one message: your name will never be truly known until you ask us for our blessing.

It is in the deflected question of Jacob that the problem can be seen most simply. Even when Jacob was wounded, he would not be turned aside from his determination to overcome his adversary, knowing full well who it was he fought. And the "man's" last, clearly ironic question closes the encounter. "Why is it that you ask my name?" "You already know yours" is the implication. And since you know yours, finally, that will be enough.

The truth was found in the sound of his own name. He had pretended that his strife was with his brother, with his father-in-law, with neighboring bandits — with anyone and everyone except the God of his dreams. Here in the wrestling match of Jacob's imagination the truth is finally set free. "I hold my brother with a trembling hand. I hold my sister with a trembling hand. I shall not let them go." It is God with whom you strive. The power of God struggled with the idol constructed in the mind of Jacob: the "real" God had to appear in the myth as someone other (a being of mystery) and yet as someone familiar (the last of a series of angels who had manifested God to Jacob).

As James Baldwin said, in a most eloquent challenge to all the Jacobs (sisters and brothers of the angels, every one of them) of America:

> The price the white American paid for his ticket was to become white: — and, in the main, nothing more than that, or, as he was to insist, nothing less. This incredibly limited not to say dimwitted ambition has choked many a human being to death here: and this, I contend, is because the white American has never accepted the real reasons for his journey. I know very well that my ancestors had no desire to come to this place: but neither did the ancestors of the people who became white and who require of my captivity a song. They require of me a song less to celebrate my captivity than to justify their own.[5]

Of course, the story of Jacob and the angels of Yahweh is only partially the story of cultural realities in America. There have been far too many denied and stolen inheritances in the history of the Americas for one culture to effect the transformation that the story prefigures. And the Jacob-which-is-America has yet to ask a blessing from any of its adversaries. How the myth resolves itself is, after all, considerably dependent on the humility of Jacob.

And the resolution of the myth brings us to the reason for this extensive meditation on "We Are Climbing Jacob's Ladder" and "Wrestle on Jacob." Unlike the majority of other groups of African American Christians in the United States, black Catholics have little opportunity to absent themselves from the life of the larger church. When African Methodists were denied basic justice, civility, and respect, they could form the African Methodist Episcopal Church and remain Methodists in good standing. So also was it true for African American Baptists, Presbyterians, Unitarians, and so on. For those in the Catholic traditions (Roman, Anglican, or even, by extension, Lutheran), to be a member of these respective faith-traditions meant that African Americans could never exercise autonomous control over their worship services. Centralized authority shaped worship and, to a great extent, therefore, the culture of the church communities.

In the first part of this study, a map of what would be "authentically black" has been drawn for our reflection and instruction. In the remaining sections of this book, major themes affecting the reality of African Americans being "truly Catholic" will be explored. African American Catholics have been, so far in American history, a part of the larger Catholic church, and have had to contend with externally imposed definitions of valid worship and authentic modes of exercising "the faith" (which are most often sanctions supporting cultural expressions of piety and tradition which are traditionally comfortable for those doing the impositions).

Wrestling matches erupt everywhere there are African American Catholics. Definitions that have been settled for hundreds of years in other African American worship communities are refreshed in battles continually. If the notion of "authentically black" *and* "truly Catholic" can ever be unified, then Jacob, Rachel, their children, and a host of heavenly witnesses are going to have to sing the same songs, from the same motives. In what remains of this study, the themes of prophetic witness, appropriate liturgical expression, recruitment and retention of vocations to religious and clerical life, and the exercise of the ministry of leadership within the faith-community will be explored.

The themes of the first part of the book will be applied to the discussions which follow. The arguments will develop "organically," it is hoped, from the interpretations of African culture that derive from drum-and-dance-based religious expression; from mystical forms of prayer; and from the sense that all of creation contains the power of the divine and that this power is to be used for healing that which has been wounded, for the restoration of balance to that which has been perverted and distorted.

Part Two

TO FEAST
AT THE
WELCOME TABLE

Chapter Three

To Go in the Wilderness

> I'm going to eat at the welcome table,
> Oh, yes I'm going to eat at the welcome table
> some of these days hallelujah!

While it should be obvious by now that the black and un-known bards, the "soldiers of the cross," determined their own liberation and fought battles more real and more washed in sa-cred blood than any metaphor of the walled city of Jericho can conjure for our imaginations, we must be cautious in how we visualize their prophetic journey out of the wilderness of slav-ery, oppression, enforced silence, and perceived primitivism. A deep, elemental clash of cultures — a clashing of visions of world and kingdom — is also a part of the story being told here. And the articulation of this cultural struggle can begin with an-other geometric figure added to that of the circle (the Kongo cosmogram).

Make Straight in the Desert

Western European and American theories of social develop-ment and some of the implications of a hierarchical view of reality (harking back to the "great chain of being") impel most of us under their sway to look forever to the new, to move away from the past, to evolve and perfect ourselves and our institu-tions, and to slough off the old, the incomplete, the vestigial. We were, so this argument might assert, at point A in our past, and we are tending/moving/hastening toward point Z. Wherever we *are*, there are still many more points for us to achieve, in our quest for the horizon of our existence and purpose. If there can be a theology of the dance- and drum-inspired circle, then we ought to be able to devise a meditation on the theories of evolution, progress, and the hierarchies of power that can be conceptualized by a *straight line.*

The dark side of such a philosophy of progress has, of course, been played out throughout much of human history. Foundational lessons of Western history concern the Persians, Greeks, and their contemporaries hacking away for advantage throughout the lands bordering the Mediterranean. We are taught about the Goths and Visigoths sweeping through Europe and northern Africa during the early centuries of the first millennium, and then about the Arab tidal wave that washed across Africa and Europe a few centuries later. Finally, we add to all of this stories of the domination of the "Indies," the Americas, Asia, and Africa by the British, French, Spanish, Portuguese, Dutch, German, Japanese, and Americans from earlier centuries to the present day. "Manifest destiny," the "white man's burden," "colonialism," and "imperialism" are terms that suggest what happens when one group of people standing on point A decide to move on to point Z, and others are standing on points of the line in between origin and destination.

For many, the definitive illustration of the phenomenon of flattening out all obstacles in the pursuit of perfection remains the legions and bureaucracies of the Roman Empire. Rome stands alone in such a history of progress. And the legacy of Rome has been an essential part of the inheritance of the Roman Catholic Church and all of its descendant churches. The value of the inheritance of these structures and mandates for conquest has been debated from the days of Constantine — and by none more strenuously than those who have found themselves on the intervening points between A and Z.

Staying with the imagery for a few moments more, we might engage in a consideration of the theories of "either/or" and of how so much of our thinking is based, from classical logic to modern mathematics, on this binary opposition of simple factors. If the truth be admitted, "adult" argument seldom moves beyond the childish, "Is so. Is not. Is so. Is not. Is. Not. Is. Not...." While many of us would pretend to more sophistication, our reliance on such rhetorical structures in what passes for political and journalistic debate would belie the argument and might embarrass us. We can find myriad examples of the modern world's dichotomous construct of itself.

Even more insidious than examples of "divinely sanctioned" domination of the always "inferior" ("noncivilized") other, or the various forms of dialectics that seem to shape all modern discourse, are the theories of *scientific racism* that settled upon the world of learning in the eighteenth and nineteenth centuries. It was the origin and *development* of the species, after all, that so captured the minds of the biologists, anthropologists, and philosophers of Europe and America from the age of the Enlightenment right up to the contemporary resurgence of studies into the supposed genetic differences of peoples.[1]

The historical narrative that would follow from this "cosmology of the straight line" has significant implications for how we will conceive of *church*, and how we will gather into community. The dialogue of many voices that should be the fount of all cultural development is often reduced to "one-upmanship" (and the term is used advisedly), and conversation transforms itself into agonistic struggles for the last word. After all, there can be only *one* word uttered at any *one* time. Either... or. Even worse is the suppression of the voices of those who are under threat of domination or eradication in the name of progress (whether it be benevolently or irresponsibly rendered); that, indeed, is a part of a global tragedy in modern times.

Much of what is being played out in this musing is directly connected with what we would call "the American obsession." History is, in this obsession, a problem to be gotten away from. After all, the new (American) covenant or compact or anointing of those who declared the "new world" to be new, and the wilderness to be "Eden," declared in such an act of appropriation that whatever went before — or whatever was present at the time of the appropriation — was of no consequence whatsoever.

Paradise, by definition, was utterly and eternally *new* — that is, radically opposed to the old.

The Americanism of the nineteenth-century transcendentalists (and other displaced romantics) cannot be understood without studying this obsession with being as nearly perfect in newness as possible. Ralph Waldo Emerson, in his call for the American scholar and poet, prepares us for Walt Whitman and his proclamation:

> Strangle the singers who will not sing you loud and strong. Open the doors of the West. Call for new great masters to comprehend new arts, new perfections, new wants. Submit to the most robust bard till he remedy your barrenness. Then you will not need to adopt the heirs of others; you will have true heirs, begotten of yourself, blooded with your own blood.[2]

Ignoring the fact that Whitman saw himself as the robust bard with sufficient generative power and creativity to parent a numberless host of poetic offspring all by himself, we can hear a quite familiar, "American" attitude in this sentiment, one that has been part of how America has sung itself from the first days of its self-discovery. "The new, the new," goes the cry. Whatever has gone before are the ruins of the past, the rubble of false starts and incomplete strivings. Each new generation, each new cultural variation, is obligated to make a straight path into the future, bringing with it only the distilled essence of the past. The heirs of Emerson and Whitman are male and female, young and old, rich and poor, and of every ethnic construction: to be an American means to be begotten of one's own blood.

It is this ever-unfolding progress, the sense of the inexorable absorption of the past, that informs what was alluded to in this study's earlier reading of "O Black and Unknown Bards." The anthropology that provides the context for this poem (perhaps all anthropology, by the very nature of the discipline) presumes that the culture under study is about to pass away from human reach — except insofar as it is recorded by more sophisticated observers. Much of the development of African American literature and culture is devoted to capturing the last remnants of the old days. Perhaps no one displays the impulse to memorialize the African American past better than Jean Toomer:

> O Negro slaves, dark purple ripened plums,
> Squeezed, and bursting in the pine-wood air,
> Passing, before they stripped the old tree bare
> One plum was saved for me, one seed becomes

> An everlasting song, a singing tree,
> Caroling softly souls of slavery,
> What they were and what they are to me,
> Caroling softly souls of slavery.[3]

Toomer, Charles Chestnut, Paul Laurence Dunbar, W. E. B. Du Bois, James Weldon Johnson, in literature, joined the legions of amateur anthropologists and musicologists who sifted through the rural areas of the South and paid close attention to the ever-more congested Negro areas of the swelling cities, collecting songs, stories, anecdotes, and narratives of the way of life of the formerly African enslaved — a way of life that would otherwise vanish with only the merest trace. This impulse to collect fragments of the African American past culminated, of course, with the massive WPA undertaking, during the 1930s, of interviewing many surviving former enslaved.[4]

The act of choosing to remember the past is the initiating incident in creating this literature or in defining this culture. The past has to be retrieved in order to be handed down. This dynamic did not necessarily have prominence in the late nineteenth and early twentieth centuries, when the overwhelming need to define themselves (and their brothers and sisters) as human seemed the highest priority for most of the African American social and cultural leaders engaged in political activism and literary productions. Claiming a usable past became one of the motives of the leading lights of the so-called Negro Renaissance. The "new Negroes" of Alain Locke's sighting were busily collecting as much of the "old" Negroes as they could find, and it is a measure of their importance that much of the

literature of contemporary African American devising owes content, style, and methodology to the pioneering efforts of people
like Zora Neale Hurston, Arthur Schomburg, Langston Hughes,
Sterling Brown, and, once again, Jean Toomer, whose master-
piece (*Cane*) owes some of its importance to it being both an
elegy and a harbinger.[5] The very act of Toomer's attempt at
capturing the "parting songs of slavery" allowed subsequent generations to benefit from the culture and to make use of what
was retained. In another way, the notion of medicinal objects
(*nkisi*), things which are useful for the health of the community,
is applicable here. In another western African tradition, that of
the creation of *adinkra* cloth, one of the more powerful images
is that of *sankofa*, an African word bearing the idea of "renaissance," a word meaning "to return and fetch that which has been
discarded or lost."

It is not at all coincidental that at the very time Jean Toomer
was seeking to record the echoes of the era of slavery, and others
were in an urgent quest for the songs, stories, and other cultural
signs of this supposedly vanishing time, European artists and
theorists were engaged in their own seismic shift of consciousness. *Cane* (1923) is as much a signpost of the emergence of a
hunger for an African American past as *The Wasteland* (1922) is
a sign of the fragmentation of culture eventually known as modernism. While both Jean Toomer and T. S. Eliot may have been
in agreement in their belief that the past was becoming increasingly unknowable, their respective texts have nurtured radically
dissimilar progeny.

Lest some romantic excess be allowed to color this discussion, it must be said that history and its values have been a
source of much anguish and conflict for African Americans as
much as for any others who must confront the fact that, for
almost all people, everywhere, "the center cannot hold." Grappling with history is part of the process inherent in becoming
an American, part of the "price of the ticket," as James Baldwin would say. The sons and daughters of outlaws and petty
criminals became the landed gentry of colonial America (English, Spanish, and French). Heretics, outcasts, and the branded

became the definers of religious and cultural standards in the new Eden. Guerrilla fighters in the woods and swamps of the North American continent eventually became the veteran patriots of liberty and the conservative adjudicators of civil "rites" and responsibilities during the early years of the Republic.

And few saw the contradictions. To be an American meant that one had the jealously regarded right to start over, as often as necessary, in the quest for a presentable self. There was limitless wilderness in which to stake a claim and an infinite horizon against which to cast one's dreams and aspirations. Unfortunately, this process of becoming American meant that one had to adapt to certain cultural signifiers which were applied with a relentless zeal. In order to be American, one had to have a position concerning the "red savages" and the "black brutes," the "heathen Chinee," and the "despicable Mexican." In order to be American, one had to go through the transformation of becoming *white* (and male, and with property, if the process is to be spelled out completely) — and *human,* that is, a person with full rights and privileges, both those that are God-given and those that are a priori granted by the state.[6]

To be an American meant that one had to re-vision one's history with all the creativity found in the biblical narratives which justify the status of "chosen people" for the children of Israel. The myths of Americanism are too numerous to mention here, but we must give serious attention to the way in which, for all its vaunted celebration of the great high holy days of secular piety, America has a poor sense of its own history.[7] As a counter to the religious imagery traditionally used by those who speak of America's divine appointment with destiny, we might say that America's Christian piety is hollow at the core in part because those who would define the nation as beloved of God forget that the beginning of all claims to heirship with Christ is found in the great Jewish invocation: "Remember O Israel...how we lived in the land of Egypt, and how we came through the midst of the nations through which you passed" (Deut. 29:16). The "chosen ones" are enjoined to also remember that because of God's mercy toward them, they are obligated to care for the widow, the orphan, and the stranger among them, and to provide for those who are enslaved under their power. Over time, being chosen came to mean, more often than not, being radically different from the widow, orphan, stranger, or enslaved, and being morally superior to them all, if not materially better provided for.

At the end of the Civil War, many African American leaders — meaning those relied upon for public articulation of the concerns of the African community in America — urged the newly liberated to step smartly into the future, leaving behind the trappings of their degradation and oppression. Many thousands took up the call, clamoring to be Americans as fully (and as quickly) as possible. The new wine of freedom needed to be placed in new wineskins of culture. Almost instinctively, the shape-shifting effort to change the importance of the past took its seductive toll on many Africans who wished to be Americans. "Emancipation" brought with it a sense of shame concerning the past centuries of enslavement.

The enthusiasm of "Free at last, free at last; thank God Almighty, I'm free at last" pulled many into a whirlwind of forgetting. Years after the early days of emancipation, James Weldon Johnson and his brother, J. Rosamund, sought to heal the breach caused by the rush to forgetting when they proclaimed in "Lift Ev'ry Voice and Sing":

> Keep us forever in the path, we pray.
> Lest our feet stray from the places, our God, where we met thee,
> Lest, our hearts, drunk with the wine of the world, we forget thee.[8]

Weldon Johnson is suggesting, in this lyric, that the principle of *sankofa* is already necessary for the African American community. Much was lost along the way, in the rush to cross over Jordan's stream. The circle was hammered into a straight line of progress, and there were few voices to stay the many who wished to forget the old ways. Perhaps the most poignant example of this determination to "move on up, a little higher," can be found in the story of the founding of the Fisk Jubilee Singers.

Every Valley Shall Be Exalted

The nine young women and men who comprised the first Fisk touring choir in 1871 resisted strongly the idea of singing their songs [slave songs] in public. One important reason was their belief, based on experiences with whites, that their music would be ridiculed and perceived as simpleminded or "primitive." Some of the students also wanted to forget the songs reminding them of the horrors of slavery; all except one member of the group... had been born in slavery. Accordingly, Isaac Dickerson, Green Evans, Benjamin Holmes, Jennie Jackson, Maggie Porter, Thomas Rutling, Ella Sheppard, Minnie Tate and Eliza Walker began their tour in October of 1871 with a concert program consisting of classical choral works and popular folk tunes; no spirituals were included.

— As told to Arthur C. Jones, *Wade in the Water*

The likelihood of ridicule and shame, the embarrassment of the past: these are the ingredients for a diminution of esteem that could have far-reaching consequences for individuals and for groups. The musical director of the Fisk Jubilee Singers, Professor George L. White (also the school treasurer), argued and cajoled (and maybe even prophesied on the matter), but to no avail. Only when the singers themselves became discouraged and disillusioned, because of the lack of support and positive response to their concerts, were they willing to reconceive their repertoire. The Fisk Singers had been organized and taken on tour in order to raise funds to complete construction of the Fisk College campus. With their original repertoire their effort was a grand failure, with small audiences and pitifully meager receipts.

As the story is told, while the singers were waiting in the back of an auditorium in Oberlin, Ohio, hoping for a chance to be included in a musical program, a lull occurred in the stage performances. Professor White gave the Fisk Singers the cue to begin singing one of the old sacred songs, where they stood. The music of their heritage took over the assembly, and

> history had now been made. The singers, encouraged by the positive audience response, sang on and on, one spiritual after another. Contrary to their apprehensions there was no sign of ridicule. The extraordinary power of the music, much of which had not been heard before in a public arena, appeared to counteract the prevailing negative racial atmosphere.... The experience at Oberlin marked a historic turning point for the students from Fisk.[9]

On their next tour, which took them to various European capitals, the Fisk Jubilee Singers collected more than twenty thousand dollars for the building of their school.

Several points should interest us in this story of the Fisk Jubilee Singers. At first, their shared shame overwhelms them and prohibits them from performing their collective task. Shame leads to depression. Depression leads to further failure. When the past intervenes, in the form of their sacred music being sung from the back of a darkened auditorium, the singers and the assembled listeners are healed. The singers go back and fetch what they would have gladly lost, and the listeners are challenged to rethink the stereotypes that prevailed so easily as to deny the singers any formal place on the program. While it is true that "history had been made," what is more important for our purposes is that history had been *restored*.

History, in the sense that we are using the term, does not connote long years or many eras. The years between 1865 and 1871 cannot be considered historically significant, in length. In terms of events, and consequence, however, those years were of great significance: passage of the Thirteenth, Fourteenth, and Fifteenth Amendments to the U.S. Constitution; and the great political experiment of Reconstruction, quickly followed by the backlash (what an ironically appropriate term) of "redemption," the *de*-construction of the political and social advances wrested for themselves by black people and their white allies.[10] In this brief but momentous period, the women and men of Fisk College, and their contemporaries, would have had hundreds of reasons to wonder what it took for them to get from the shores of the Jordan and to set up camp in the "promised land." The days of Jubilee were "nasty, brutish, and short," in other words.

Knowing full well the dis-ease and suffering that came with emancipation, the Fisk Singers had justification for wishing to step away from the pain. By returning to fetch what they were in danger of discarding (even for the most rational of psychological reasons), these black and known bards healed themselves and provided a model which could be employed for generations to come. They healed themselves through a radical confrontation with the doubts and feelings of shame that they had interiorized over a lifetime of debasement. But they were able to do more than see clearly through a dark glass — they chose to wade in the water of their circumstance and make a way to Gilead. They survived a part of their past and they were restored, coming full circle. Both the conflict and the Fisk Jubilee Singers' choice of solution to the conflict are part of the legacy we have inherited.

Another Fisk student added his perspective to the dilemma faced by the Jubilee Singers, and his articulation of the problem facing them, him, and their descendants has in itself become a cultural heirloom. W. E. B. Du Bois composed one of the most sacred black texts in history when he wrote in *The Souls of Black Folk:*

> [T]he Negro is a sort of seventh son, born with a veil, and gifted with second sight in this American world, — a world which yields him no true self-consciousness, but only lets him see himself through the revelation of the other world. It is a peculiar sensation, this double-consciousness, this sense of always looking at one's self through the eyes of others, of measuring one's soul by the tape of a world that looks on in amused contempt and pity. One ever feels his two-ness, — an American, a Negro; two souls, two thoughts, two unreconciled strivings; two warring ideals in one dark body, whose dogged strength alone keeps it from being torn asunder.[11]

While the sacredness of this "canonical" text is justified by almost a century of citation and approbation, we must read it fresh with our own eyes and notice that the tension, the essential conflict, articulated by Du Bois is exactly the same as reported about the Fisk Jubilee Singers some years before Du Bois's matriculation at Fisk.

One of the first things we notice, in comparing Du Bois's romantically conceived struggle with the disillusion and sense of shame felt by the Fisk singers is that the singers found a third way to conceive of themselves. By their faith, by their returning to the sacred music composed in just such conflicted and oppressive moments as those evoked by Du Bois, the singers were able to see themselves from a third perspective. The Hegelian dialectic so often employed in Du Bois's writings is challenged by the singers looking at themselves as "children of God." To be bound for "*the* kingdom" is slightly different from striving to take one's place in the "kingdom of culture," as Du Bois would argue at the time when he was writing *The Souls of Black Folk.*

The salvific insight came to the singers in the dark recesses of a room where they were not welcomed. In the darkness, in their recurring sense of exile, they reacted with the trained reflexes of their own cultural integrity. They sang themselves into the light. "Anybody ask you who you are, who you are, who you are; Anybody ask you who you are, tell them you a child of God." That identity has more promise than the (seeming) binary opposition expressed by Du Bois. In fact, Du Bois does not entirely subscribe to his own argument. He does not say that the essential conflict between being an American and being a Negro ends in destruction of the self. On the contrary, he says that it is the Negro's "dogged strength alone" which keeps him from "being torn asunder."

Whence cometh this strength? The thoughts are fused in the realm of the spiritual; the unreconciled (Jacobean) striving finds its resolution in claiming an identity in the kingdom of God, and the warring ideals are brought to truce by the introduction of ideals forged in "the great camp-meeting in the promised land." For a people who trained themselves to wade in the water, and to transgress the rolling of the Jordan River, which "chills the body, but not the soul," the development of a soul of incomparable power to withstand even the contempt and pity of the oppressor should not be surprising. It should be expected.

Du Bois presents a subtle version of this "way out of no way" in the passage just quoted. It is unlikely that many of his original readers would have appreciated the sly way in which Du Bois introduces the old "African" ways, the unreconstructed folkloric tradition of the mystically empowered "seventh son of the seventh son, born with a caul over his face," into this otherwise lofty meditation on the tragic struggle to become human.[12] Du Bois does not elaborate upon the figure; there is no need. As is true of many other African American authors writing to a multi-faceted audience, Du Bois performs this act of *signifying* (an allusive cultural reference possessing several — sometimes contra-dictory — simultaneous meanings) and allows it to create an act of rhetorical subversion.[13] He has entitled the book, *The* Souls *of Black Folk*, thereby emphasizing the inner integrity and author-ity of black people. The careful reading Du Bois gives to African American religious practices, and his assured claim that the prac-tices of the Negro in America are connected with the rituals of Africans on the continent, have set standards for all subsequent studies in this field. This moment, with its offhanded assertion that some magic power keeps the Negro soul from being torn asunder under the relentless assault of racism in America, is a moment rarely given adequate attention.

With all of the sophisticated research and intellectual endeav-ors in which he was so long engaged, Du Bois was profoundly affected by his encounters with the Negro church of the ru-ral South. His journey from his birthplace in Great Barrington, Massachusetts, to the campus of Fisk in Nashville, Tennessee, carried him as far as any of the other great hegiras he under-took in his long and complex life. Neither Boston, London, Heidelberg, New York, nor Accra held any more revelation for his understanding of black spirituality than did his sojourn through rural Tennessee while an undergraduate at Fisk. In this, he presents himself as a model of how African Americans can undergo a "*sankofa* journey" in order to complete a spiritual, emotional, and cultural circle. When he arrived at Fisk, he was, he says, "thrilled to be for the first time among so many people...of such various and extraordinary colors...who it seemed were bound to me by new and exciting and eternal ties."[14] Later in the same autobiographical reflections, he makes explicit those eternal ties when he answers the great question posed by Countee Cullen, in his poem "Heritage": "What is Africa to me?" Du Bois's response to that question seems as pertinent today as when it was articulated:

> [A]s I face Africa [in 1940] I ask myself: what is it between us that constitutes a tie which I can feel better than I can explain?...[O]ne thing is sure and that is the fact that since the fifteenth century these ancestors of mine and their other descendants have had a common history, have suffered a common disaster and have one long memory. The actual ties of heritage between the individuals of this group, vary with the ancestors that they have in common and many others: European and Semites, perhaps Mongolians, certainly American Indians. But the physical bond is least and the badge of color relatively unimportant save as a badge; the real essence of this kinship is its social heritage of slavery; the discrimination and insult; and this heritage binds together not simply the children of Africa, but extends through yellow Asia and into the South Seas. It is this unity that draws me to Africa.[15]

The contradiction between the negative heritage and the joyous claiming of that inheritance is a part of the composition of "blackness" as a cultural signifier, be it found in the blues, in black sacred song, or in popular music and comic monologues. Du Bois was ever careful to remind his readers that "race" was a concept, not a biological fact.[16] He was adamant, also, in reminding those same readers that race was as real as the lynch-tree, and often just as deadly. Nevertheless, he declared himself a "race man" all through his life (and died a guest of the state and an honorary citizen of Ghana).

The "one long memory" is redemptive, is healing, becomes
an *nkisi,* to be handed down with great reverence to each suc-
ceeding generation. The "second sight" of the seventh child of
the seventh child is not to be understood in the usual meaning
of prophetic sight. The mystical visions induced in this reading deal with the *past.* To seek and to find strength and hope
and power and possibility and solutions to the intractable problems and crises of one's present life, one must go back. The juju
and conjuring suggested by this cultural prescription involve the
dance of hope enjoined in "The Sermon on the Warpland," by
Gwendolyn Brooks:

> And went about the warpland saying No.
> My people, black and black, revile the River.
> Say that the River turns, and turn the River.
>
> Say that our Something in doublepod contains
> seeds for the coming hell and health together.
> Prepare to meet
> (sisters, brothers) the brash and terrible weather;
> the pains;
> the bruising; the collapse of bestials, idols.
> But then oh then! — the stuffing of the hulls!
> The seasoning of the perilously sweet!
> The health! The heralding of the clear obscure!
>
> Build now your Church, my brothers, sisters.[17]

"Doublepod" and "double-consciousness" are offered as qualities of perception that make anyone more human, more sophisticated, more situated for transcendence. These are highly
intellectual permutations of the dance cultures of western Africa translated into a peculiarly *American* experience. We are once
more being instructed in the need to dance to more than one
drum at the same time. These Africans taking root in the United
States continue to demand that all pay attention to their vir-
tuosity, their ability to be on the ground and way up on the
mountain; to be singing with a sword in their hands; to be pray-

ing in the valley and wading in the water and swinging away in
the chariot of Elijah — all at the same time.

By never permitting their horizon to be circumscribed by
the accidents of historical oppression without countering with a
resistance found in the claim of kingdom and eternity, the self-
anointed heroes of this story knew very well "who defines the
terms by which we live." Everyone involved in our existence is
part of the process of defining these terms. One aspect of the
genius of black folk is that the circle was adjusted to find room
for the divine intervention that they considered to be a constitu-
tive part of the definitional performance. A few lines later in the
same poem, Gwendolyn Brooks has the preacher of the sermons
"on the warpland" offer this injunction:

This is the urgency: Live!
And have your blooming in the noise of the whirlwind.

This is an apt way of presenting the quality of engaged mysticism that has been the subject of this study. Unlike the voice of
God that appears to the prophet Elijah in the stillness after the
wind, the earthquake, and the fire (1 Kings 19:11–13), the prophetic encounters of African Americans have always been in the
water, in the fire, in the flood, in the upheavals and the calamities
of life. As the old gospel song says, "God leads us along, in the
night season and all the day long." That song is but a variation on
the older spiritual which asserts a radical humility for the singer
when it states that "I've been in the storm so long, Oh, give me
little time to pray." Note that neither song says to God, "Take
away the storm, the calamities." Each song — and the spirituality
that informs it — asks for the strength to go through the experience without losing connection with God. Black spirituality, old
and new, concerns itself with transcending difficulties, not with
avoiding them. While this is true of all forms and practices of
spirituality, to some extent or another, it must be asserted that
black spirituality (in this reading, at least) has an organic conflict with any form of religious expression that seeks to ignore
the calamitous aspects of history; that seeks to avoid dwelling
on the disruptions and upheavals of personal and public endeav-

ors; that holds the maintenance of good order and discipline to be higher priorities than the manifestations and re-creations of those events where God is most present.

In other words, a spirituality that sustains a people as they "conduct [their] blooming in the noise and whip of the whirlwind"[18] will be in open conflict with those spiritualities that privilege the private experience of the encounter with God. Private piety can support a relativism that could be more "American" than "Catholic," and more secular than ecclesial. Solid rock is replaced with shifting sand. The claims of "self-evident" truths are placed in opposition to that which is (or has been) commonly held — and the private could become more important than the communal. Many of the wars waged over liturgical renewal, the sustenance and development of parish faith-communities, and the recruitment and retention of vocations to religious and priestly life can be seen within the frame of this conflict of spiritualities. The *doubleness* found in this reading of black spirituality allows only a *seeming* contradiction. Within black culture, and throughout African American history, overwhelming evidence can be found to support the claim that African Americans are "bilingual" in their abilities to navigate among differing cultural expectations.

From popular folklore to the most profound of the black sacred songs, the understanding is almost universal. The sentiments in the following two selections are more similar than one might suppose at first glance. Both are concerned with the withholding of full knowledge and the use of masks in a situation where survival depends on delayed gratification.

From the "secular" world:

> Got one mind for white folks to see.
> 'Nother for what I know is me;
> He don't know, he don't know my mind.
> When he see me laughing
> Just laughing to keep from crying.[19]

From an adjoining pew:

I got shoes, you got shoes, all God's children got shoes;
When I get to heaven gonna put on my shoes,
And walk all over God's heaven.
Heaven, heaven;
Everybody talking 'bout heaven ain't going there.
Heaven, Heaven;
Gonna walk all over God's heaven.

In order to build a church, one must join with others who possess, among other things, a similar vision of God, world, humanity, and covenant. And the group must have common expectations of behavior and accountability to which all who would be a part of the circle must give assent. The creed must be supplemented with other covenantal statements, and one's initial assent must be renewed in the presence of fellow believers and confirmed often. The building of a *black* church will entail, first, the recognition that standing in the "promised land" might mean standing on sand and not on solid rock. It might mean a careful investigation of whether the so-called Jordan River of promise and redemption might be taking those who navigate through it on a journey into psychic destruction and spiritual deprivation. Even when the journey seems like a straight line aimed at isolation, alienation, and cultural impoverishment, those who would be sanctified, called holy, can always change the rhythm of the dance in which they are caught up. "Say that the River turns, and turn the River," is an injunction for all who would be black and Catholic, and for all those who cannot find unity of desire and accomplishment in circumstances that often seem beyond their control and in situations which may appear outside the power of their ability to define terms that will be inclusive enough for them to put on their shoes *before* they get to heaven.

Claiming heaven might seem an immodest act, especially in a country whose cultural *mythos* has been so deeply affected by notions of Protestant sobriety and probity. The rituals of self-effacing humility are still practiced by politicians, athletes, entertainers, and heroes no matter how ironic the situation or context. Black theology, as expressed in "I Got Shoes," provides another interpretation. Declaring that "I got shoes," even though I may not get to wear them until I am in heaven, and asserting that the claims of others to a place in the kingdom might be proven hollow at the Day of Judgment can be regarded as the acceptance of good biblical theology, singing out the inclusivity of the parables concerning those invited to the wedding feast.

This song subverts the hierarchical perspective of those who would assign citizenship in the kingdom only to those who have manifested good judgment in business, sober living in the home and in the community, and (among a host of other possibilities) equanimity in disposing of a portion of the blessings of God to those who are less fortunate. "I Got Shoes" also subverts the presumption that well-ordered behavior should be normative in times of worship. And for the purposes of this study, the song gives wonderful proof to the argument that black theology must begin with the heritage texts of black sacred song.

This tradition of black theology — composing songs that will heal, sustain, educate, and transform — begins with the appropriation of scripture. The songs interpret biblical stories by supplying a perspective of involvement in the dramatic elements of the stories and re-creating the sacred events in transformative ways. The heroes called up in the songs are present in the worshiping community. The injunctions and commands of God are made compelling once more to those who would renew themselves as the children of God. The behavior of the first chosen and of the early members of the church is reenacted in the performed songs and sermons, bringing down the liberation of the Exodus and the fire of Pentecost upon the assembled believers.[20]

The song "I Got Shoes" appears in many forms and under many titles. Various material objects appear in different versions of the song, all adding up to an inclusive vision nurturing a song about inclusion. We shall use the version found in *The Books of American Negro Spirituals*, edited by the brothers James Weldon and J. Rosamund Johnson. The version they collected is called "All God's Chillun Got Wings," and their title adds to this discussion of prophetic performance. The items included in the list of God-given possessions are robes, wings, harps, and shoes.[21]

(Other versions add "crowns" to the list.) The combination of the homely and the apocalyptically grand, shoes and wings together, bespeaks the poetic genius and the hard-eyed mystical realism that have been discussed throughout this study. Earth and heaven are united in the song. The joyous realization that the deprivations due to enslavement, oppression, extreme poverty, and persecution are only a part of the picture of being a child of God allows the believers to "keep their hands on the gospel plow," to quote another song. "To walk all over God's heaven" (or sing, or shout, or fly all over heaven) has several plausible interpretations, none of which need be considered in conflict with the others. For those who would see this song as a masked "escape" song, using heaven as a metaphor for the North, or for freedom in a geographic sense, the ability to walk anywhere without requiring an authorization from an "owner" is a condition devoutly to be desired. For those who see the song as a meditation on the distinction between all earthly limitations, to be fulfilled only in the completeness of heaven, the song tells of "a great gittin'-up morning" that all would avidly seek.

There might even be another consideration, based on a verse that is often added to songs that deal with "singing and shouting" in heaven (including some versions of "Hold On"): "When I get to heaven, gonna sing and shout, be nobody there to turn me out." The ability to fly all over heaven, or sing all over heaven, or shout all over heaven, might have a connection to whoever would limit the behavior, the performance, of African American spirituality to those acts that were subdued, quiet, and controlled by the official ministers of worship. There might be some merit in considering that some of those who sang "When I get to heaven I'm gonna put on my wings and shout all over God's heaven" were challenging some of their own fellow worshipers (when Bishop Daniel A. Payne sought to rid the AME church of those who would sing "cornfield ditties," he was called an agent of the devil for his efforts to control the singing and the order of worship). Oppression can be found in the church as well as in the marketplace and in the fields. Many spirituals deal with those who "talk about heaven" but who are not going there. In the various gospel accounts of Jesus' encounters with those who would inhibit the inclusivity of the kingdom, strong condemnations are bestowed on scribes, Pharisees, and even, sometimes, disciples.

One such account of a warning to those who would too narrowly conceive of righteousness (for that is what the song "All God's Children" is about, ultimately) can be found in Luke 14, where Jesus presents his picture of the "welcome table": "When you give a banquet, invite the poor, the crippled, the lame, and the blind. And you will be blessed, because they cannot repay you, for you will be repaid at the resurrection of the righteous." When Jesus finishes this statement, a guest at the gathering says, "Blessed is anyone who will eat bread in the kingdom of God." This prompts the telling of one of the great parables of generosity and inclusion. "Someone gave a great dinner," we are told, and many of the originally invited sent their regrets. "Then the owner of the house became angry and said to his slave, 'Go out at once into the streets and lanes of the town and bring in the poor, the crippled, the blind, and the lame.'" In this account no one needs the proper attire; they need merely show up. When this first harvesting of the public roads has been completed and there is still room at the table, the owner of the house then orders the slaves to "go out into the roads and lanes, and compel people to come in, so that my house may be filled." Then, in a conclusion that speaks strongly of the justice of God, the owner says, "For I tell you, none of those who were invited will taste my dinner" (Luke 14:13–24).

It should take very little imagination for us to see how this story would be a centerpiece of the theology of liberation that is found everywhere in black sacred song. "Everybody talking 'bout heaven ain't going there." Volumes could be filled with the accounts of the enslaved Africans who would have worshiped God in the sanctuary but who were denied access by their supposedly Christian "owners." Some were beaten repeatedly for their attempts; some were disfigured, or maimed, or chained to trees, in order to put a halt, literally, to their efforts to be a part of a worship circle. Enslavement made many a man, woman, and child lame, blind, and crippled. Many others, when they became

ill or infirm or too old for productive labor, were put in wagons
and driven from the plantations into the nearest cities, where
they were dumped on the streets and made homeless. Any of
these oppressed people who would have heard this story would
have had no difficulty in appropriating the good news as it was
proclaimed by Jesus: you have a place at the welcome table.[22]
(And those who inflicted such evil upon you won't be there.)
For some, we must always remember, the stories of scripture are
not metaphorical, but all too painfully descriptive. "But then oh
then! — the stuffing of the hulls!" The people who composed
"All God's Chillun Got Wings," and all who added their own
variations to the song, and those who continue to sing it with
fervor and understanding today, have all seen a great light: no
matter your condition, God has room for you in the kingdom
of righteousness. "Sooner or later a change is gonna come," they
said. And it did.

The welcome table and the dance circle announce the same
sacred space. It is also the "hush harbor" and all those other
places where Jubilee is celebrated. In order for there to be harmony and well-ordered behavior — without which there can be
no dance, no hospitality — there must be a recognition that all
those who gather have a right to be there, that the invitation
alone is enough for citizenship in the kingdom, and enough for
the right to choose a seat and sit down. Even more, the invitation, implying a close, familial, relationship with the Almighty,
precludes even the necessity for well-mannered behavior. Once
it has been realized that "You got a right, I got a right, we all
got a right to the tree of life," then all manner of demands can
be made.

The "right to the tree of life" and the invitation to choose a
seat in the kingdom are based on the prodigal generosity of God,
not on the merits or hard work of the one being invited. In fact,
it should be noted that in the theology of the old black sacred
songs, the demands for righteous behavior can just as readily be
made of God, as they might be asked of the believers. It is hard
to imagine any other established form of Christianity allowing
the confrontational sentiments of:

Sit down, servant. (I can't sit down.)
Sit down, servant. (I can't sit down.)
Sit down, servant. (I can't sit down;
My soul's so happy, Lord, I can't sit down.)

That ain't all you know you promised me;
Promised me a long white robe and a pair of wings.

Go over yonder, Angel; get my servant's wings.
Place them on my servant's frame; now,
servant, do sit down.

Sit down, servant. (I can't sit down.)
Sit down, servant. (I can't sit down.)
Sit down, servant. (I can't sit down;
My soul's so happy, Lord, I can't sit down.)

That ain't all you know you promised me;
Promised me a starry crown and a golden harp.

Go over yonder, Angel; get my servant's crown.
Place them on my servant's head; now,
servant, do sit down.

Sit down, servant. (I can't sit down.)...[23]

This song carries the drama of being invited to a great feast
much further than could be imagined from reading the account
of the wedding feast in Matthew (22:1–14), or the account just
discussed, in Luke 14. Being invited, getting to the feast, finding
a seat: "That ain't all you promised me." All of God's children
may have shoes, robes, crowns, harps, and wings; some of them
will settle for nothing less than everything due to them from
the promises of God. This is part of the theology of liberation
that seems absent or suppressed in most interpretations (especially those that are more Marxist-inspired in their reading of
culture and in their understanding of what it means to be a
person), perhaps because there is little recognition of the great
humor and relational intimacy felt by the believers who claim
these songs.

Recognizing the starting point of dance, of song, of art, in the faith statements of a people, of a praying community, takes us to different strategies and conclusions when we study how this specific people liberated themselves from oppression and degradation. Unlike most other versions of liberation theology, black theology has historical confirmation for its claims. "Once we were slaves, exiles, motherless children a long ways from home," this theology tells us. "And then we decided to steal away, to the lonesome valley, where we could cry out in our great need, 'Come by here, Lord, come by here.'" When God heard the cry of the poor, they were delivered. And there was a day of Jubilee. The captives were set free. In history. It *was* "a great gittin'-up morning," indeed. The fact that Jubilee was quickly replaced with more toil, suffering, alienation, and death cannot be denied. But since God's mighty hand "delivered Daniel from the lion's den, Jonah from the belly of the whale," and the black and unknown bards and their sisters and brothers from Pharaoh's enslavement in America, we must be humble in the presence of a faith that says it will surely happen again. "God gave Noah a rainbow sign, no more water but the fire next time."

The remembrance of that covenant-price is life-giving. The utter certainty of having shoes, and all the other accouterments of heavenly citizenship, brings to the believer the power to make things happen, including the power to push oneself into the room where the wedding feast is taking place and then to ask to be served.

Interlude

Steal Away to Jesus

On Thursday, July 9, 1992, at 7:30 in the evening, the doors to an exhibit hall of the New Orleans Convention Center were opened, and the delegates and guests of the Seventh National Black Catholic Congress were finally allowed to enter the space. Much argument and confusion had preceded the opening of the exhibit hall doors. Many delegates had been wandering around from meeting to meeting, or from one store to another, or had walked a considerable distance from hotels and restaurants and were ready to sit down and get themselves situated for the evening's eucharistic liturgy. More than four thousand people were expected for the Mass, and since it was the opening liturgy, since it was New Orleans, and since the Black Catholic Church had high hopes for an "all-stops" celebration, folks were not amused at being told to stand in the lobby and be patient.

The volunteer ministers of hospitality, all experienced and sensitive church workers, were not happy, either, at being asked to be gatekeepers and traffic guards, instead of being able to display the gracious, inclusive, welcoming style that is the hallmark of New Orleanians at their best. Most of those who were ready to begin the celebration were, indeed, *ready*.

When the congress liturgist (myself) finally gave the signal to the musicians, the ministers of hospitality, and the ushers that the gathering rite could move to the next stage, the excitement, anticipation, and curiosity of the whole community were as high as they could be before they turned into negative grumbling and criticism. People began to fill the space, climbing up into the bleachers which had been placed to form a true arena, risers facing the center of the room, from all four sides. The seats stretched up into the darkness; the lights were as dim as could be maintained without endangering the safety of the assembly; the room was devoid of most decorations, save that of the colorful attire of the congress delegates who had done their part for the liturgy by dressing as if they were illustrating the Psalm which declares that we are "wonderfully, fearfully made." The vibrancy of a truly multicultural church sparked high levels of energy in the exhibit hall within a very few minutes.

And what did the assembly see when they settled into their seats? First, and most importantly, they saw each other. When they looked into the room, they saw that they were part of a vast enclosing — four thousand people looking at each other across an almost bare and humble floor. For the only objects present in what should have been the "sanctuary" for the eucharistic liturgy were a large carved wooden *Corpus,* suspended from the ceiling, hanging directly centered in the middle of the air, and three overturned iron pots on the otherwise bare floor. Trees and plants ringed the space and formed aisles through which the assembly had passed, when entering the hall. Trees; iron pots; and a wooden figure of Jesus, hanging in the air. And the people of God, gazing upon their own vibrant, expectant selves.

The liturgy had begun, surely and well, even before there was any formal announcement of the fact. When the drums began a slow and gentle rhythm, the ordained ministers were brought into the hall. The deacons, priests, bishops, archbishops, and cardinals of the church marched into the room, to the drum call, and they bowed, as ministers always do, to the form of Jesus hanging there for all to see. And in their bowing they looked at the three overturned iron pots, the bare floor, wondering, I am sure, where the altar was, and what they would witness, and whether it would be a eucharistic celebration that would be called *valid* and *proper* by those who must ascertain such things.

When the majority of the clergy were seated, the "ministers of the preparation" entered the hall. Forty women entered, from each of the quadrant points of the circle. The women marched into the hall, slowly, deliberately, in cadence. Each of the women carried a long and heavy palm branch, which had been collected during the previous day from all over New Orleans. The women were well-rehearsed in the disposition of the palms. They swung the branches on a count of "four," and on each fourth beat, they dragged the palms across the floor, in a ritualized sweeping of the bare space. Like women from all over the South, for generations, they came to the clearing to prepare it. In those places where there was nothing but dirt in the front yard, the women of the South would sweep the dirt, making it level and fresh, and then they would sprinkle water over the swept area, tamping down the dust and creating a semiglazed surface. Some would drag rakes through the dirt, forming intricate patterns. Arranging the earth for the ritual is an important part of the preparation.

This act of sweeping out the space where the liturgy would be performed symbolized, also, the need to start at the bottom and be attentive to whatever was distracting or impure in the environment. "Sweep the place clean. Get rid of the demons that might hinder us," all were told. And the women dragged the heavy palms against the floor, one, two, three, sweep. After the women had progressed a half-rotation around the circle, the choir began to softly whisper, "Hush," on each of the dragging beats of the palm branches. One, two, three, "Hush." One, two, three, "Hush." The choir continued this whispering for several moments, and then added, *a capella*, the words to the great hymn:

> Hush, hush, somebody's calling my name.
> Hush, hush, somebody's calling my name.
> Hush, hush, somebody's calling my name.
> Oh, my Lord, oh my Lord, what shall I do?

When the women had moved around the enclosure, they were followed by twenty more women, each carrying a plain galvanized tin bucket, containing water. They moved around the space, damping down the dirt, settling and cooling off the area. The choir continued singing, with their voices alternately swelling and dropping according to the spirit of the room.

Ten men then arrived with the wooden components of an altar, which they quickly and efficiently built in the middle of the space, directly below the form of Jesus, and directly over one of the overturned iron pots. Once the people had assembled, and the clearing had been prepared, it was time for the building of church. The welcome table had to be set up. Young women bearing bowls of incense then entered the space, ushering in the men who were the African American Catholic bishops. Each of these men was attired in authentic Ashante cloth, imported from Ghana and reserved for the most solemn of occasions. When the bishops had been led to the altar, the women, young and old, walked in a circle of blessing around them, sprinkling them with the water, and honoring them with the incense:

> Hush, hush, somebody's calling my name.
> Hush, hush, somebody's calling my name.
> Hush, hush, somebody's calling my name.
> Oh, my Lord, oh my Lord, what shall I do?

The assembly was then led in chanting a litany invoking those who are called "the black saints." When this prayer was finished, the eucharistic liturgy proceeded as usual, with singing, praying, preaching, Communion, and missioning of the people. Authentically black? Truly Catholic? Our history teaches us that African American worship begins in the clearing, in secrecy. Long before African American Christians (Catholic or otherwise) either built or inherited houses of worship, their ancestors connected the *utilitarian* with the *holy:*

> On one Louisiana plantation, when "the slaves would steal away into the woods at night and hold services," they "would form a circle on their knees around the speaker who would also be on his knees. He would bend forward and speak into or over a vessel of water to drown the sound."
>
> The most common device for preserving secrecy was an iron pot or kettle turned upside down to catch the sound.
>
> ...[A]t the core of the slaves' religion was a private place, represented by the cabin room, the overturned pot, the prayin' ground, and the "hush harbor."[1]

In order to make use of these core rituals, one does not have to be black or Catholic. Many black Protestant congregations are searching for ways to "return and fetch that which has been lost" (*sankofa*). Many liturgists and many who are part of church assemblies that are hungry for ways to revitalize their worship look for any insights and methods of preparing services that speak to the whole person, and speak as completely as possible to the demands of the world through which we sojourn. In order to make use of these principles, we must be willing, first and foremost, to allow ourselves a "Patmos" experience (Rev. 1:9–10) and to be lifted up to see a new heaven and a new earth, as St. John the Divine was gifted to see. And then we must be willing to return and build our vision where we stand.

Chapter Four

Sometimes I Feel
Like a Motherless Child

I, John, your brother who share with you in Jesus the persecution and the kingdom and the patient endurance, was on the island called Patmos because of the word of God and the testimony of Jesus. I was in the spirit on the Lord's day and I heard behind me a loud voice like a trumpet saying, "Write in a book what you see and send it to the seven churches." —Rev. 1:9–10

What does it mean to be black and Catholic? It means that I come to my church fully functioning. That doesn't frighten you, does it? I come to my church fully functioning. I bring myself, my black self, all that I am, all that I have, all that I hope to become, I bring my whole history, my traditions, my experience, my culture, my African American song and dance and gesture and movement and teaching and preaching and healing and responsibility as gift to the church. —Sister Thea Bowman

Doing Our First Works Over

The two epigraphs above may serve our reflections as the "pillar of cloud by day and the pillar of fire by night" that guided the Hebrew children through the desert (Exod. 13:21). John the Evangelist is an important figure in black theology, appearing often in the sacred music. It is John's mysticism, and not any particular vision recorded in Revelation, that is the major focus of many of the references. "I want to walk in Jerusalem just like John" is indicative of the apostle's place in the sacred circle of holy ancestors. His was a prophetic mysticism. Not only was he lifted up, spoken to, shown visions. He was also instructed to "return and tell what you see." Prophecies must be shared with the people. The heart of biblical prophecy is a call to conversion. The prophetic message of Jesus and the apostles and evangelists who spoke to the early Christians is "revelatory" in this special way: "Behold I make all things new" (Rev. 21:5). When all things are truly made new, old assumptions and premises are no longer operable. The elect inhabitants of the New Jerusalem will be sustained by new wine in new wineskins. The "wedding feast of the Lamb," as it is described in Revelation, harks back to the parable of the supper that we have already seen in Luke 14:

It is I, Jesus, who sent my angel to you with this testimony for the churches. I am the root and the descendant of David, the bright morning star.

The Spirit and the bride say, "Come."
And let everyone who hears say, "Come."
And let everyone who is thirsty come.
Let anyone who wishes take the water of life as a gift.
—Rev. 22:16–17

This invitation, if applied seriously to issues concerning black Catholics during the development of the Catholic Church in the United States, would be a two-edged sword of judgment held against those who have been responsible for the guidance of the church. Far too often the story of African Americans who wished to be a part of the Roman Catholic Church could have taken as its theme the song Sr. Thea Bowman sang to introduce her 1989 speech to the Catholic Bishops: "Sometimes I Feel Like a Motherless Child." The rich, complex history of African American Roman Catholics in the United States has begun to be told in other places, by gifted scholars.[1] What concerns us here are a few significant issues that must be fearlessly faced if

black Catholics are to heed the call of the black Catholic bishops
to become Pentecostal evangelizers of ourselves, and if our sister
and brother Roman Catholics are to heed the prophecies of Jesus
and his disciples, who tell us: only the bridegroom is allowed to
determine who sits at the welcome table.

The first issue is that of *confronting the false premises*. The
refuge of the church, the inviolate integrity of "sanctuary" —
a place where no harm can befall an individual, a place where
perfect welcome, perfect support, is unconditionally given — has
seldom, if ever, been the experience of black Catholics in the
American church. In fact, in those places where the enslavement of Africans was the economic foundation of society and
where the beneficiaries of that enslavement were Roman Catholic, the Africans who were black and Catholic served, more often
than is admitted, as the "living endowments" of the Catholic
Church in the United States. In *The History of Black Catholics in the United States*, Father Cyprian Davis, O.S.B., shines
the light of painstaking (and pain-giving) scholarship on the issue of the worth of African men and women in the building
of the American Catholic Church. To use only one example,
Davis says:

> Many bishops were slaveowners. Inevitably some of them
> did engage in the buying and selling of slaves, just as many
> priests and religious did. The attitude toward slavery, how-
> ever, was not uniform. John Carroll, the first American
> bishop, was a slaveowner. He claimed that he had no slaves
> of his own, but he did have in his service a slave lent by his
> sister and a servant to whom he gave a salary.[2]

John Carroll's distinction between "owning" and "using" undoubtedly came from his understanding of the vow of poverty
as it would have been practiced by him and his fellow members
of the Society of Jesus. Property dedicated to the maintenance
of the community would not have been the personal possession of any one member of the community. In his position as
superior of the Jesuits of Maryland, and in his role as the first
English-speaking, native-born bishop of the United States, John

Carroll had the responsibility of caring for the property of the Society of Jesus and, later, of the diocese of Baltimore. Both Davis and he are correct. He was a "slaveowner," in that he had the legal right to acquire and dispose of real property; and as a member of a religious order dedicated to poverty, he had nothing for his personal use. His governance of, and disposal of, enslaved subjects were for the common good. (This is a distinction that would be employed for decades in the Society of Jesus, and in other religious communities, both male and female.)

Using some of the experiences of the Jesuits to illuminate the notion of "living endowments," we can see that North American missionaries shared some of the relativism displayed by the great Bartolomé de Las Casas. Because of his fierce, single-minded devotion to the cause of "New World Indians," Las Casas urged the Spanish Crown to abolish the practice of enslaving the indigenous peoples of Mexico and to replace them with captured Africans. Later in his life Las Casas expressed his bitter regret at having urged such a compromise, and (as Cyprian Davis acknowledges) he was himself never responsible for the importation of Africans as slaves into the Americas. What concerns us, though, and what cannot be abrogated by the most compassionate of interpretations, is that Las Casas was able to make such a suggestion in 1516 because he shared the general cultural assumptions of those in the highest realms of authority: throughout much of Europe at the time, the Moor, the "black," was on the lowest link of the great chain of being. Africans, due to their color, their perceived cultural differences, their long domination of the Iberian Peninsula, and their non-Catholic beliefs, were ripe for whatever negative circumstances could befall them or that were imposed upon them by war or other means of subjugation.[3] In this regard, Las Casas was of the same mind, early in his life, as his contemporary, Ignatius of Loyola, the founder of the Jesuits. In the second chapter of his autobiography, Ignatius recounts his famous encounter with a Moor, while traveling to Montserrat. After a lengthy discussion on the lifelong virginity of Mary, and after feeling a sense of futility because he could not convert the Moor to his way of thinking, Ignatius "thought he had done wrong in allowing the Moor to say such things about our Lady and that he was obliged to defend her honor. A desire came over him to go in search of the Moor and strike him with his dagger for what he had said."[4] The future saint then employs a rudimentary "discernment of spirits," allowing his mule to guide his actions: if the mule follows the trail of the Moor, Ignatius will kill him. If the mule ambles on toward the shrine of Montserrat, the "pilgrim" will spare the Moor's life. The mule went toward the shrine.[5] The utter simplicity with which Ignatius accepts the mule's guidance (directed, he is certain, by the providence of God) is remarkable in and of itself. The ease with which he contemplates killing the Moor for the imputed dishonor of the Virgin is consistent with cultural attitudes in sixteenth-century Spain, and those attitudes informed the way the Catholic Church comported itself for a long time to come — and not only in Spain. The relative worth of a Moor's life is what we pay attention to, here.

This relativism regarding the worth of another, enslaved, human's life permeates Roman Catholic institutional concerns for most of the history of the United States. The great Jesuit missionary efforts toward working with Native Americans in the Mid- and Far West, from 1823 on, was based at Florissant, Missouri. In writing about this period of American church history, Kenneth P. Feit has this to say:

> From the onset... the blacks who worked the [Florissant] farm served as a means for reducing labor demands so that Jesuits could catechize Indians. The fact that these blacks had their own spiritual needs was recognized, but no special effort was put into evangelizing neighboring black populations.... A combination of factors subtly developed among the early Jesuits an acceptance and (indirectly) an endorsement of the inferior status assigned the black man, even under the Indian.[6]

Many nuns and priests, and many of the congregants of parishes in Maryland, South Carolina, Georgia, Alabama, Missouri, and Louisiana, sustained themselves with the economic benefits gained from the labor of — and the sale of — enslaved Africans. In his study of the ambivalent feelings Jesuits in Maryland had concerning their reliance on slaves, Edward F. Beckett, S.J., discusses the emerging consensus, in the early 1800s, regarding the necessity of selling the slaves owned by these Jesuits:

> In considering the motives for selling the province's slaves, the most obvious of explanations should not be overlooked — money. The Jesuits had previously sold slaves for financial reasons, in order to pay debts, for example. [The provincial, William] McSherry's major argument for the sale of the slaves also involved finances. But there was an additional reason for his enthusiasm — the schools. For McSherry and others, the Jesuits had to choose between the farms and the schools.[7]

In those instances where the church (clerical, lay, and religious) focused its efforts on the evangelizing of the Africans in the community, the efforts would have been severely compromised by a set of assumptions that would have denied any African Catholics full membership in the church. The underlying assumptions concerning the humanity of, the spiritual and social value of, and the possibility of salvation of enslaved Africans have not changed much over the history of the Catholic Church in the United States. Since some of these assumptions still retain their potency in the contemporary church, they are worth these moments of reflection. They are the shackles that bind the thinking of Catholics, white, black, and other, concerning the place of black Catholics in the church. Until these shackles are studied, they cannot be broken; and none of the captives will go free.

In the minds of the apologists for slavery, and in the minds of many who were opposed to the institution of slavery, these African men and women were, variously and all: savages, marked with the "curse of Cain" (black skin), and made inferior by the incomprehensible justice of God; they were placed upon the earth to be "servants of their brothers," as fulfillment of the "curse of Ham." They were assigned to the lower orders of subhumanity, with more affinity to primates than to the apex of the races, the white man; and in this regard, they were especially given over to licentious behavior and sexual promiscuity of every possible fantasy. They were judged incapable of self-discipline, sobriety, ordered passions, or philosophical reflection. The act of enslavement, at its — by the enslavers — perceived best was an opportunity for the African subhuman savages to be brought under the benevolent rule of those who would civilize them (as best as they could), sanctify them (as far as they were able, without freeing them), and protect and care for them (as long as it was economically feasible and socially permissible).[8]

Much of the pejorative thinking can be located in two of these areas. These two areas shelter some of the deepest roots of racism and alienation that have affected the experience of black Catholics in the United States, no matter their legal or clerical status. The first is the long association of blackness with *evil* and *sinfulness*. Several of the scholars cited previously give detailed analyses of this identification of color and negation. A comment from *Begrimed and Black,* by Robert E. Hood, will suffice for our discussion now. Before he presents an extensive reading of the thoughts of Origen, Athanasius, and Jerome on the link between black skin color and the condition of sinfulness, Hood introduces his theme with the following summary:

> Evil represented chaos and nothingness as potent forces in a power struggle that goes on cosmologically and on earth. Hence, blackness as a visual reminder was both a sign of the primal inferior being of the devil fallen from the light of Christ and a sign of cosmic disorder and nonbeing. Blackness meant malevolence. Cultures and peoples stained, even allegorically, with this mark of privation were thus seen as an outward and visible reminder of the threat of nonbeing and annihilation of the good, at least in the Latin fathers.[9]

Hood continues his study, adding references to a variety of early Catholic figures who visualized temptation, evil, and seduction in images of black men, women, and children. From Augustine and Ambrose to Hildegard of Bingen, these Catholics saw black people as the embodiments of sin, imperfection, and disease ("the black plague"); and blackness was the color of the enemies of Christ, the color of the devil and of his spawn.[10]

The second, and closely related, area of pejorative thinking which has had enormous negative consequences for African Americans in general, and mostly explicitly within the Catholic Church, is in the area of the *demonization* of African sexuality. It would be impossible to summarize the vast literature that has been produced to discuss this issue. Much of American literature has this specter of blackness at its core. Much of popular American culture, from the early days of its colonization, has an almost adolescent fascination with fantasized projections of black male and female sexuality.[11]

Hood has a provocative (and, to my mind, altogether convincing) summary of this theme also. Hood argues:

> I think that for most Europeans carnality with regard to blacks was what the nineteenth century called an "elixir of repression" whose origins can be traced to Greco-Roman times, early Christian theological influences, monasticism, and Christian ascetics.... Erotic ideas about blacks provided Europeans a convenient way of venting their negative societal view of blacks, while at the same time allowing them a discreet indulgence in exceeding existing taboos about engaging black flesh.[12]

After Hood cites several explicit "indulgences" (physical descriptions of blacks provided by European travelers), he carries his discussion into the Americas, where (citing Winthrop Jordan) he focuses on the early, frightening reliance on black male castration as a punishment. He writes that several colonies, and several islands in the West Indies, had statutes permitting male castration as a punishment particularly reserved for black males, only occasionally used on Native American slaves:

> Castration was considered a means of subduing "spirited" black males who were suspected of violating white

women. The purpose was to control their sexual prowess, not dissimilar to what was done to bulls and stallions. Furthermore, castration was linked to carnal curiosity about the black male's phallus, a legacy from ancient Greek and Roman society.[13]

Hood's explanation here of the rationale for the castration of black males is, of course, only a partial explication of the root of the phenomenon. The legal prohibition against sexual behavior was also fed by the stereotypes and prejudices that were, as Hood suggests, the legacy of centuries of European pseudo-science and theology. The "curiosity" that Hood finds in the European mind is connected to the long-lived practice of projecting onto the despised "other" those conditions and obsessions found within the subject harboring the fixation.[14] This, too, is part of the legacy of early Christian ruminations on blackness, carnality, and evil. And these ideas, themes, and projections are part of the legacy of all who would call themselves *American* and *Catholic*. No one is exempt from the influence of culture.

Therefore, the denial of the false premises which undergird this set of cultural perceptions and assumptions must engage all who would be concerned with the development of faithcommunities that are "authentically black and truly Catholic." And such a grappling with these premises will be a struggle as eventful as the war waged in the heavens between the angels of light and the angels of darkness.

In this regard, Sr. Thea Bowman's speech to the National Council of Catholic Bishops becomes a guiding testimony, a prophetic call to conversion. "I come to my church fully formed," Sr. Thea said in essence to the bishops. "My church" and "fully formed" are not concepts that come easily to the lips of black Catholics (or any other practicing Catholics), and are certainly not concepts that have fallen like dew on the desert when heard by many clergy and administrators of Catholic institutions.

From what has been discussed so far it should be easy for us to see that the long history of imputing a "stain" to dark skin color would cause many to doubt that any African American could possibly be "fully formed" (wholly human) or that African Americans could ever be considered worthy of full membership in the Catholic community. Much of the history of this "real" Catholic Church (white, European) in its dealing with those who it judged were not as blessed by God with full human qualities has been the story of admittedly great, heroic men and women engaged in bringing a message of truncated hope and severely modified blessings to those they knew could never taste the fullness of the kingdom for which they themselves were bound. For all too many African Americans, Hispanics, and Native Americans in the United States, the evangelization offered them has been as much a burden as a blessing, in its open ambivalence and obvious incompleteness. A story told in the Gospel of Mark has some poignancy here:

> [A] woman whose little daughter had an unclean spirit immediately heard about him, and she came and bowed down at his feet. Now the woman was a Gentile, of Syrophoenician origin. She begged him to cast the demon out of her daughter. He said to her, "Let the children be fed first, for it is not fair to take the children's food and throw it to the dogs." But she answered him, "Sir, even the dogs under the table eat the children's crumbs." Then he said to her, "For saying that, you may go — the demon has left your daughter." So she went home, found the child lying on the bed, and the demon gone. (Mark 7:25–30)

"Sometimes I feel like a motherless child, a long ways from home." Indeed. When Thea Bowman presented herself, in 1989, before the Catholic bishops of the United States and turned the story of the Syrophoenician woman into a blessing and a challenge, she confronted basic assumptions and premises on several levels, simultaneously.

Bowman, the "master drum dancer" from Canton, Mississippi, became more than an evangelizer to herself and to her people. She subverted centuries of ministry to the colored, Negro, black, African, African American members of the Catholic

Church in the United States. For the duration of her address, the bishops became guests at her table and had to share the meal of salt, tears, bread, sorrow, humor, and hope that has long been the real banquet of blackness in America and in the church. Thea Bowman said that she was fully formed and quite comfortable in the church, knowing full well that some in her audience felt that their invitation to her was extraordinary — particular to her and to her unique situation. That was the first level of challenge, the place where we see the first premise denied. Her *essential validity* was not determined by her doctoral degree; her record of research and teaching; her tenure in vowed religious life; her celebrity. Nor had she "arrived" because she had been invited to appear before the Catholic bishops on several occasions. Her feet were planted on the solid rock of her culture, as she described it in the passage we have quoted. But what did she present to her audience? And what do her words do for us, today, as we contemplate the difference between the "Syrophoenician" experience of most African American Catholics and the sense of freedom displayed by Thea Bowman in most of her public life as a teacher, evangelist, and prophet?

Perhaps some of her freedom and some of the fire that drove her on her relentless journey to "tell the true truth" had their source in the fact that she was born into a positive, supportive, and deeply religious community and became a Roman Catholic after her basic spiritual and social formation had been achieved. In many ways, the persona she assumed for much of her later life, the old lady from rural Mississippi, filled with folk wisdom and the rawest of poetry and the simplest of spirituality, was an evocation of the foundation of her earliest years. We must remember that she left Canton, Mississippi, for the far different climate (in every sense of the word) of La Crosse, Wisconsin, at a relatively early age (sixteen), but that she had already achieved a full maturation in her culture.[15] A child of the black Baptist Church, Thea Bowman, the nun, would have had a very different attitude toward her role in the life of the church community than might be manifested by others who had been socialized into very different understandings of "church." She, like many of her sister and brother African American Catholics, could live with her Protestant heritage, her black cultural riches, and her Catholic identity without finding any contradictions in the blending and harmonizing that would have had to be done for a sense of holistic integrity. The *Protestant* quality of all African American worship needs much further exploration (as did the "Catholic" nature of much of black theology, as we saw in the first part of this study).

Without reducing an epoch of revolution to simplistic generalities, it is not impossible to conceive of the movements known generally as the Protestant Reformation as, among other phenomena, an attempt to confirm in the heart of each and every believing Christian that the institution called "church" was indeed their own possession; and once they had been touched by a personal relationship with the Holy Spirit and with Jesus the Savior, they were as formed as they needed to be for full participation in the work of the church.[16]

Much of the success of Protestant evangelization among Africans during the earliest days of colonial America might in part be attributed to the possibility of Africans, enslaved or otherwise, experiencing admission to Christian fellowship with a guarantee that they would be received with the understanding of Paul: "No one will be justified by the works of the law, [but by] faith in Christ" (Gal. 2:16). Such scriptural references fueled the revivalism in the North American English-speaking colonies, from Georgia to Massachusetts, beginning with the work of the Wesleys and their cohorts, especially George Whitefield.[17]

Not many years passed before the churches that welcomed Africans among their members, and where many of these Africans were respected leaders of the community, shifted their theology into a blemish of disfiguring compromises that marks many denominations to this day. In the early fervor and the frenzy of the eighteenth-century Pentecostal moments, evangelizers might have believed with all their hearts the truth of the proclamation: "There is no longer Jew or Greek, there is no longer slave or free, there is no longer male and female; for all of you are one in Christ Jesus" (Gal. 3:28). But no matter the integrity of such a preachment, by the time some influential Anglican, Methodist, Presbyterian, and Baptist theologians had reflected on the exigencies of slavery as the engine which guided all economics and politics in America and in England, the text of evangelization and conversion had been practically reduced to:

> Slaves, obey your earthly masters with fear and trembling, in singleness of heart, as you obey Christ; not only while being watched, and in order to please them, but as slaves of Christ, doing the will of God from the heart. Render service with enthusiasm, as to the Lord and not to men and women. (Eph. 6:5–7)

It was in response to this perversion of the gospel, and because of the deep need to build upon the cultural foundations that made sense to them, that the uncounted bands of African worshipers decided to steal away to Jesus and call him into their midst in the hush harbors in the wilderness. When the promise and the premise of their *essential validity* was turned into what Frederick Douglass would later call "slaveholding religion," and the African converts were reduced to second- or third-class status in churches where they had previously served as exhorters, deacons, and evangelists, they exercised their Protestant option of dissent.[18] They walked. They walked into their own space, and made it sacred. If belonging to a church which was redefining itself into a "white church" would lead to a deformation of their self-regard and humanity, then they would choose to separate themselves from the *unrighteous* and re-form themselves into a worshiping community wherein they could control their spirituality, their rituals, their education, their singing, and their finances. It was this impulse to "start over, from the ground up," that fed the founding mothers and fathers of the independent congregations built in the eighteenth century from Georgia to Pennsylvania.[19] "I got a right to the tree of life," they sang.

"Rejoice in Hope, Be Patient in Suffering, Persevere in Prayer" (Rom. 12:11)

Be Patient

The political and social organization of the Protestant churches in America (with the exception of the Church of England, which never departed in its essential organizational structure from that which it inherited from the Church of Rome) generally permitted decentralization of authority and local and regional autonomy. Such structural preferences favored the establishment of independent black churches. Being Protestant gave adherents the right to follow the promptings of their hearts and to affiliate with like-minded believers who wished to worship with as much independence as they could maintain and still remain in agreement with the denominational creeds of their respective churches. The heroic Richard Allen provides compelling testimony on this point. When Allen and his fellow African congregants, no longer able to endure the "scandalous treatment" of them by the white Methodists of St. George's Church, decided to finally build their own house of worship, he was forthright in asserting his commitment to remain faithful to the teachings of Methodism. Richard Allen, Absalom Jones, and their fellow African dissidents were opposed to the white Methodists' betrayal of their own moral code. When challenged by one of the more influential elders in Philadelphia to desist in his efforts to raise money to build a separate church, Allen had this response:

> We asked him if we had violated any rules of discipline by so doing. He replied, "I have the charge given to me by the Conference, and unless you submit I will read you publicly out of the meeting." We told him we were willing to abide by the discipline of the Methodist Church, "And if you will show us where we have violated any law of discipline of the Methodist Church, we will submit; and if there is no rule violated in the discipline we will proceed on...." We told him we were dragged off of our knees in St. George's Church, and treated worse than heathens;

and we were determined to seek out for ourselves, the Lord being our helper.[20]

This confrontation took place in 1787. When Allen was writing of this incident in his autobiography in 1833, he also presented to his readers a testament of fidelity to the principles of Methodism that is as beautiful today as when it was composed:

> Notwithstanding we had been so violently persecuted by the elder, we [Allen and Absalom Jones] were in favor of being attached to the Methodist connection; for I was confident that there was no religious sect or denomination would suit the capacity of the colored people as well as the Methodist; for the plain and simple gospel suits best for any people; for the unlearned can understand, and the learned are sure to understand; and the reason that the Methodist is so successful in the awakening and conversion of the colored people [is] the plain doctrine and having a good discipline.... I feel thankful that ever I heard a Methodist preach. We are beholden to the Methodists, under God, for the light of the Gospel we enjoy; for all other denominations preached so high-flown that we were not able to comprehend their doctrine. Sure am I that reading sermons will never prove so beneficial to the colored people as spiritual or extempore preaching.... We would ask for the good old way, and desire to walk therein.[21]

Fifty years after the founding of the African Methodist Episcopal Church, Richard Allen continued to discern the difference between the creed and its sometimes unworthy adherents. He and his cofounders of the AME Church underscored their fidelity to their "awakening" with their famous moral code: "God our Father, Christ our Redeemer, Man our Brother." As another old song says, "You may talk about me just as much as you please. / I'll talk about you when I get on my knees."

As was true throughout Europe, Catholicism in America took a very different attitude toward "fidelity to the discipline." Dissent was not possible. To dissent from authority was to declare oneself no longer a member of the church. One could not dissent from behavior that was tyrannical and racist by establishing an independent, racially secure, Catholic worshiping community. On the surface, to be a Catholic meant, then and now, that one had to endure all manner of suffering for the sake of Christ and remain within the "fold." The centralized authority of the Catholic Church, based on the hierarchical flow of power from the top of the church down, allowed African Americans no departure from one existing subsidiary institution (be it parochial, diocesan, or national) for the sake of forming a semi-independent or semi-autonomous institution.

In fact, African Americans were historically denied the privilege granted other cultural groups in exercising the Catholic variation on the establishment of independent congregations. The phenomenon of "national churches" was partly a positive recognition of the validity of cultural components in worship and partly a pragmatic compromise. Nevertheless, culturally based parish communities were allowed great freedom and greater autonomy than contemporary Roman Catholics (many of whose ancestors were part of these parishes) are often willing or able to remember. The urban landscape of the United States is dotted with the relics of ethnically driven worship: German churches, Polish churches, Irish churches; Lithuanian, Bohemian, Sicilian, and Piedmontese Catholics had close-knit and autonomous social communities, and they put up the schools and the churches needed for the spiritual confirmation of their ethnic and religious identities. African Americans were the recipients of missionary evangelization and, as such, were directed into worship communities that were deemed appropriate by external determination. Often the best and most humane compromise black Catholics could expect, in the face of being treated "worse than heathens," was the establishment of a separate chapel for their use, to be staffed by the same clerics who pastored in the "real" (white) church. Such oppressive treatment ranged from segregated worship spaces, to the denial of the sacraments, to the segregation of cemeteries, to the withholding of adequate instruction, and to the absence of compassionate and consistent pastoral care.

"Sometimes I feel like a motherless child," Sr. Thea sang. Father Joseph M. Davis, S.M., writing during a time of black Catholic renaissance, sums up the ideas presented here when he says:

> The fundamental concept of the Church's mission in this country distinguished between *ordinary and extraordinary.* The ordinary work was in the white community; the extraordinary was in the black community. Church personnel functioning from this viewpoint conceived of their task as converting, in the full sense of the word, black people not only to the one, *true,* Church, but also to a "better" way of life. The subtle implication was that black people were also being converted *away from* something, and that was from a culture, tradition and heritage which was not in itself significant, valid or civilizing. The music, dance, diction, patterns of speech and manner of behaving were thought of as some kind of "aberration" from the normal or white man's style of life.[22]

The difference between national churches and "colored chapels" rests firmly on the false premise that African Americans were inferior, in all essential ways, to white Americans. The Catholic Church had been long- and well-established in the regions of Europe from which the immigrants came, and there the issue of the *essential validity* of the people was not in question. In many of these same regions, however, the overdetermined inferiority of the African had long been established as a fact of science and as the basis of commerce. As was seen earlier, the prejudice concerning *blackness* as a symbol of *sin* and *evil* permeated Christian theology and guided issues of politics throughout the medieval, modern, and contemporary eras of Europe. European immigrants had, therefore, a much easier time of becoming "white" in relationship with "black" people than is readily admitted. The seeds of racism were carried across the ocean and were germinated in the fresh and fertile soil of the Americas.

It is in this context that the second area under our review, that of the *demonization* of African sexuality, must be discussed.

During the first three hundred years of U.S. history, most of the African American Roman Catholics of the United States would have been found in the regions colonized by European Roman Catholics. The Spanish and French colonies (that later became parts of Florida, Alabama, Louisiana, Texas, New Mexico, and California) and the English-speaking Catholic regions of Maryland and South Carolina contained the vast majority of black Catholics in the United States. And each of these regions falls within the boundaries of the cultural and political territory known as "the South." Even with the great urban migrations of African Americans in the twentieth century, the majority of African American Catholics are still to be found in these traditional bases. And it is within these regions that the most horrific and systematic oppression of Africans occurred. The legally supported, and culturally and religiously sanctioned, oppression of African American men, women, and children known as *lynching* concerns us here, as it is the phenomenon of lynching that has been most often employed to defend and justify the demonization of black people in America. That lynching was targeted toward the economic, political, and social domination of the white population over their black neighbors and was not based in the supposed status of black men and women as "beast-like sexual predators" is a notion long overdue as a means of confronting long-held myths that still control much of the "received wisdom" of the American public. The mythology surrounding lynching has a direct bearing on certain assumptions that have had a significant influence on the shaping of a Black Catholic Church in the United States.

In Suffering

One of the more infamous and odious moments in Thomas Jefferson's long and influential intellectual career occurs in his discussion of the inferiority of the African, found in his *Notes on the State of Virginia*.[23] Reflecting the peculiar blend of emotion, fantasy, and speculation that all too frequently constituted the field of "scientific racism," Jefferson asserts:

The first difference which strikes us is that of colour.... And is this difference of no importance? Is it not the foundation of a greater or less share of beauty in the two races? Are not the fine mixtures of red and white, the expressions of every passion by greater or less suffusions of colour in the one, preferable to that eternal monotony, which reigns in the countenances, that immoveable veil of black which covers all the emotions of the other race? Add to these, flowing hair, a more elegant symmetry of form, their own judgment in favour of whites, declared by their preference of them, as uniformly as is the preference of the Oranootan [orangutan] for the black women over those of his own species.... They secrete less by the kidnies, and more by the glands of the skin, which gives them a very strong and disagreeable odour.[24]

The African woman is the preferred sexual partner of primates; the African (man or woman?) prefers the white person as a sexual partner. Africans are unreflective ("incapable of the higher forms of reason," Jefferson says later in this passage). Africans are predisposed to sleepy indolence, or manic disport, unable to plan for the future. Africans stink. These assertions by Thomas Jefferson have had a long and tenacious hold on the mythology of America, and the logical consequence of such thought has been bloody and relentlessly depraved. While no one can blame Jefferson for the actions of those who came after him, he can be held accountable for using the rhetoric of scientific discourse to barely mask his own distaste for African women and men.

A straight and short line can be drawn from these comments of Jefferson to the virulent demagoguery of the savage reestablishment of white supremacy in the South after the Civil War. In the midst of the usual and necessary qualifications that are the stock-in-trade of all responsible historians, we can find kernels of outrage in various descriptions of lynching. One general history of America introduces the Ku Klux Klan thus:

"Typically the Klan was a reactionary and racist crusade against equal rights which sought to overthrow the most democratic society or government the South had yet known," wrote one historian. During its brief career it "whipped, shot, hanged, robbed, raped and otherwise outraged Negroes and Republicans across the South in the name of preserving white civilization."[25]

Later on in this same study, the following comments of an Episcopalian priest pierce through the fog of time and remain razor sharp:

A young Episcopalian priest in Montgomery said that extremists had proceeded "from an undiscriminating attack upon the Negro's ballot to a like attack upon his schools, his labor, his life — from the contention that no Negro shall vote, to the contention that no Negro shall learn, that no Negro shall labor, and (by implication) that no Negro shall live."[26]

The distinguished historian George M. Fredrickson provides a gloss on this widespread reliance on violence as a means of controlling the black population of the South:

[T]he dramatic outbreak of racial lynching, as well as the series of pogrom-type race riots that broke out in southern cities between 1898 and 1907, expressed deep popular feelings. The orators and writers who fulminated during this period against "the Negro beast" or "the Negro menace" did not create this mood of "Radical rage"; they simply responded to it and helped legitimize it. The conservative image of blacks as perpetual children who would be content to remain in their "place" as useful menials was thus displaced in the collective mind of the white South by the image of the beast-rapist who needed to be held down by force as he degenerated toward extinction.[27]

Fredrickson connects both our areas of reflection in one place. The first image, that of the blacks as "perpetual children," is the image of the subhuman African eternally in need of guidance, support, and control. The second image, that of the "beast-rapist," has become the nightmare of inverted blackness that haunts white Americans and harms African Americans every-where, still, in America, be it played out in popular media (film, television, music), in professional sports (the athlete as promis-cuous criminal), or in politics (the black male as killer-beast; the black woman as uncontrolled breeder). Mary Frances Berry and John W. Blassingame spell out the white rationalizations for the hunting down of the "beast-rapists." They write:

> [T]he white South developed a monolithic assault on mis-cegenation. It began as part of the campaign to wrest control of the political structure from blacks, but the ide-ology did not emerge in its final form until the 1880s. ... Drawing on the concepts of Social Darwinism, whites expressed great fear that miscegenation would lead to an ir-revocable degradation of the superior white race.... [M]ost whites believed that blacks were so far down on the scale of humanity that the descendants of white-black unions would be low in intelligence, capacity for self-government, self-control, and morality — as well as weak, short-lived, and sterile. In short, miscegenation threatened to destroy civilization.[28]

This demonization of African Americans took place in the South, but not exclusively. All of white America had much to gain from the disenfranchisement of black people. The demonization was useful in keeping black men and women economically dependent, politically powerless, and captured in continual psychological instability. If we apply these conditions to the lives of the African American women and men who were members of the Roman Catholic Church before and during the peak of this virulence, we shall see how impossibly high were the hurdles placed before them, in their quest for a place at the wel-come table. And, also, we should be deeply moved by the heroic achievements of those who knew they were children of God, no matter how orphaned they felt.

Persevere

Knowing...that our divinely established and divinely guided Church, ever the true friend of the down trodden, will, by the innate force of her truth, gradually dispel the prejudices unhappily prevailing amongst so many of our misguided people, and therefore, anxious not to forestall in any way the time marked by God for bringing about this great work, we feel confident that this solemn expression of our convictions, of our hopes and of our resolutions, will have at least the advantage of proving that we — the Catholic representatives of our people — have earnestly contributed our humble share to the great work for whose final accomplishment all our brothers are ardently yearning.

— Delegates to the Afro-American Catholic Congress,
1889, Baltimore

Afroamerican culture is essentially African culture. The Catholic Church will remain religiously ineffective in the black community unless it can effectively syncretize African culture with Catholic worship, just as the black Protestant church two centuries ago syncretized African culture and biblical religion.

It is unlikely that this synthesis of black culture and Catholic worship can take place unless it can do so under an independent black authority in the church.

— Clarence Joseph Rivers[29]

Sixty years (1829) before the delegates assembled in Baltimore for the first Afro-American Catholic Congress, the Oblate Sisters of Providence organized themselves, in that same city, into the first officially recognized congregation of African American women religious. Little more than a decade later (1842), the Sisters of the Holy Family established themselves in New Orleans.[30] Neither group of women was welcomed into the Roman Catholic Church with widespread enthusiasm, general support, or compassionate understanding — either from their sister religious or from many of the clergy and hierarchy. How could it have been otherwise?

Both Louisiana and Maryland, Catholic colonies in their settlement, were also part of the slaveholding South. The founding of these congregations was accomplished in both cases by several women who had their family origins in Haiti.[31] The women who gathered in these pious associations were educated, accomplished, cultured examples of black womanhood. These women faced danger, oppression, enslavement, and sexual mistreatment whenever they stepped onto the streets of Baltimore and New Orleans. If technically "free" black citizens of New York and Massachusetts could be kidnapped into slavery, how much more immediate must have been the threat to African American women who had no legal rights, dwelling in communities where all black women were subject to the worst abuses imaginable. St. Paul provided the text for their lives when he proclaimed: "Love is patient; love is kind; love is not envious or boastful or arrogant or rude. It does not insist on its own way; it is not irritable or resentful; it does not rejoice in wrongdoing, but rejoices in the truth. It bears all things, believes all things, hopes all things, endures all things" (1 Cor. 13:4-7).

The patient endurance of oppression, slander, mistreatment, neglect, ridicule, and alienation at the hands of other religious communities, (at best) indifferent clergy, and hostile civic authorities did not shipwreck the determination of these women to succeed. And their miracles were many, not the first of which is their continuing presence into the twenty-first century. The spirituality of these congregations of black women religious was heavily influenced (as would be expected because of the times) by the French asceticism of the late eighteenth century. (The patient, quiet, endurance of suffering was not unique to the black women who would be vowed religious. The devotion to the Sacred Heart would have had a dominant influence on their spirituality and on the spirituality of their chaplains and patrons, all French-educated clergy.)

But even this consideration must be played out according to our theology of the drum. Patient endurance and fierce independence were both present in the founding of and the development of these communities. While the piety of the age would demand that accounts of their deprivations and abject conditions be discussed in terms of identifying with the suffering Jesus on the cross, we must also tune our ears to hear another statement: "We would rather starve in a hovel than turn our ways to decadence, degradation, and the destruction of our self-esteem as women. We would rather eat only bread at our table with all who join us than eat fine foods in places secluded from the poorest of the poor," they seem to say to us, across the years.

Several excerpts from a remarkable document in the possession of the Sisters of the Holy Family will bring the point home. Sr. Mary Bernard Deggs kept a journal in which she recorded her reminisces of the early days of the congregation. While she was not a founding member, Mother Deggs was a confidant of several of the women who were among the earliest members of the Sisters of the Holy Family, including Mother Josephine Charles, who is considered one of the founders of the community, and whose life (1812–85) spanned the first forty years of the community's existence. Mother Mary Bernard also had personal recollections of another of the founders, Mother Juliette Gaudin (1808–88). In her journal Mother Deggs offers this comment concerning an early manifestation of the "theology of the welcome table," as it applies to the spirituality of black Catholics:

> And we have had many of the grandest and richest families of New Orleans to come and live [in St. Bernard Home, opened in 1866], ... [m]any of whom have been rich and have even owned slaves in former times, and we have the mistress and her slaves in there at the same time and they lived like angels together and it is a very striking thing to see the love of them. What was one of the most striking of all was to see the mistress and her slave eating at the same table. One could not help seeing that the Lord is the master of heaven and earth. All who wish to see these persons living in that state of perfect union have only to call at the old St. Bernard and Lafon's Home on Hospital Street.[32]

The invitation for the slaveowner and the former slave to sit at the same table was not given or accepted lightly. Many criticisms were leveled against the Sisters of the Holy Family by potential benefactors or clients because of their mingling people together without regard to their social status. In Louisiana that was cause for legal and informal (but just as severe) prosecution and persecution. The Sisters, while compromising in some regards, never lost sight of the integrity of their ministry:

> One of the greatest pains for us were after emancipation was that those owners who had previously sent their slaves to us to be instructed wished us to refuse to give them any more lessons. But that was asking too much of our sisters when our dear Lord said, "Go and teach all nations." And we as sisters are more obliged than others to teach all to know their god. And the day that we would refuse would be the day of sin for us for our dear Lord said in another place that He had not come for the just but to save sinners. This would have been preaching one thing and practicing another, for the rich has many friends when they have money. We would work in vain if we were to seek to please them and to neglect the poor, for he that is in health has no need of a doctor. (7)

One need not perform an overly subtle reading in order to hear the strong call for justice in these recollections of a black woman religious in 1894. "Preaching one thing and practicing another" is a first cousin to "Everybody talking 'bout heaven ain't going there" and to "I've got to live the life I sing about in my song." Throughout Mother Deggs's journal, the reader finds dozens of similar spiritual apostrophes. At one point she says of Mother Josephine Charles: "Our dear Mother Josephine was a woman of prayer and also fear of offending her maker. Above things she loved justice" (34).

"Women of color" (as they were known in New Orleans and in Baltimore), these women religious — and their sisters of the spirit who tried but were less successful, some of them, in establishing long-lived foundations — loved justice, practiced charity, and walked humbly before all (Mic. 6:8). They had little choice. With other women religious and unsympathetic clergy demanding that they not wear religious habits; with idle and curious onlookers wreaking mischief and mayhem upon their property and persons; with laws and customs conspiring against them in the courts and in the marketplaces and neighborhoods where they sought safe passage, these women were being pragmatic in wearing the mask of radical humility and passivity in the face of unimaginable threats and downright meanness. Beneath their severe religious garb was contained the awareness of their options. Mother Deggs offers the following poetic description that "veils" an awful truth about the circumstances facing well-educated "women of color" in the Catholic South:

When [Mother Josephine Charles] was a young girl her sister...[had a] dancing master come to the house to teach, but dear Mother Josephine preferred to go to David's dancing master, that was before the altar of Christ to dance with. I say to dance with Christ, for one hour in the chapel in the presence of the dear Lord in the blessed sacrament is far sweeter than one's whole life of vanity in a ballroom, dancing with a sinful creature who is blinded by his many sins that are most hideous in the sight of Almighty God, our good father. Our dear mother said to herself, "I have a dancing master far superior to that and I you [sic] will all see him when the time will come." (33)

This bare indictment of the sexual predators controlling the world of black women in these oppressive social environments is a complement to the story told by Harriet Jacobs in her autobiography, *Incidents in the Life of a Slave Girl*.[33] Like Jacobs, Josephine Charles had to make a radical decision to avoid being scarred by sexual oppression. Jacobs chose to have children "fathered" by the "most likely" of the white men in her neighborhood, hoping that his perceived decency would provide safety for their children. Her hope proved futile, and she embarked upon one of the more remarkable responses to the sexual degradation of African women in all of our history. She falsified her escape from slavery and remained hidden from the world, for years, on her grandmother's property. Josephine Charles, Juliette Gaudin, and Henriette de Lille; their companions; the women who became Oblate Sisters of Providence; the women who lived lives of humility and service like Mother Matilda Beasley in Georgia — all made choices equally as radical as that of Harriet Jacobs. For them a life of *consecrated virginity* was an emancipation from the demonization of their sexuality, and their choices were public acts, confronting the worlds into which they were born, and from which they daily fled. Referring to these women as "mother," and to their companions in their chosen state of life as "daughters," "children," and "sisters," is more than an act of sentimental piety. What the external world would consider the absolute negation of sexuality, these women named as an act of spiritual completion.

Every act involved a series of conscious, clearheaded discernments. For those who would judge them promiscuous, nonreflective, beastlike seducers of men, these women presented themselves as more honest, more spiritually integral, and more disciplined than any of their white counterparts. The "myth of the black superwoman" is not of recent vintage. In order to sustain and protect themselves, these women religious created alliances and political affiliations with white women and men (both lay and clerical), with wealthy and well-situated free persons of color, and with a few influential members of the hierarchy, in order to receive legal and social support for their endeavors. Without their religious garb and their ascetic language, these women would be looked upon as the first African American business and professional women, the precursors of the women entrepreneurs of the Far West and the urban East of the late nineteenth and early twentieth centuries. In many places these black women religious built long-lasting institutions of education, benevolence, and social development that are the Catholic equivalents of the great institutions created by the black Protestant churches. Unfortunately, when historians survey the development of the "black churches" as black-controlled institutions, the work of these black Catholic women is usually missing. Whatever future may shape the Black Catholic Church, the centrality of these black women religious must be honored.

Part of the reason for their continued marginalization stems from the fitful emergence of black Catholic clergy in the last half of the twentieth century. That there was no comparable development of black Catholic clergy nor any complementary communities of black men religious in the nineteenth and early twentieth centuries is an issue that also demands some reflection, as we look at who is missing from the welcome table, as we confront some of the consequences of a church foundering on the rocks of false premises concerning African Americans.

In Prayer

> Now the word of the Lord came to Jonah son of Amittai, saying, "Go at once to Nineveh, that great city, and cry out against it; for their wickedness has come up before me." But Jonah set out to flee to Tarshish from the presence of the Lord. He went down to Joppa and found a ship going to Tarshish; so he paid his fare and went on board, to go with them to Tarshish, away from the presence of the Lord.   —Jonah 1:1–3

> By the power of the sacrament of orders, and in the image of Christ the eternal High Priest, they are consecrated to preach the gospel, shepherd the faithful, and celebrate divine worship as true priests of the New Testament.
>
> —*Lumen Gentium*

One of the enduring miracles of the Catholic Church in the United States, and perhaps one of its "marks" as *catholic*, is the presence of African American men who are ordained bishops, priests, and deacons and vowed religious. No matter the total number at any given period of American church history, the question should never be, Why are there so few? but rather, How can there be *any?* The preceding discussion should have made it painfully evident to the reader that the criminalization of black identity in American society has been a constant factor in the definition of "black," "white," "minority," and "other," from the earliest days of the European colonization of the Americas and the enslavement of countless millions of African men and women.

The perception that African men and women were inferior, less than human, and incapable of autonomous discipline and self-control is a foundational myth of "American" culture; and, as such, it is as present in the minds and policies of the Catholic Church as it is in the halls of Congress or in the "justice" system. No missiology which focused its efforts on what Joseph Davis called "extraordinary" ministry could easily conceive of the objects of Christian charity and service as fully sanctioned peers within the Catholic community. The full political and sociological implications of the presence within the Catholic Church of an ordained black Catholic priesthood are only rarely addressed.

When black priests address the issue, the passion of their voices so threatens the dialogue that little positive effect is achieved; and that small effect is seldom, if ever, the fault of the black voices. The prophetic voices of such men as Joseph Davis, Clarence Rivers, Lawrence Lucas; the statements of the founding members of the National Black Clergy Caucus; the proceedings of subsequent symposia, seminars, and sociological surveys are seldom regarded, beyond a notice of the "angry bitterness" contained in the utterances. As has been said before, the alternative of establishing separate congregations wherein black clergy could exercise autonomous leadership while maintaining denominational affiliation with the "mother" churches is not an option for Roman Catholic African Americans. And as long as African American Catholic communities are considered to be "mission" territories, there will be little change in the status or stability of African American men in clerical or religious life.

Similar to the devastating stereotypes that abused the African American women who wished to form religious communities in the nineteenth and early twentieth centuries, the cultural myths (that renew themselves like the head of the allegorical Hydra) concerning black men are legion; and they are just as demonic.

This mythology tells us, among other things, that black men are lazy, dishonest, infantile; are prone to violence; are in need of constant supervision; are sexually promiscuous and obsessive; are intellectually substandard and psychologically unstable. These characteristics of black male behavior have been touted as scientific evidence and as justifications for everything from peculiar and absurd medical treatments in the early nineteenth century to excessive and totalitarian punishments in the judicial system in the late twentieth century. This list of characteristics (and many others that could be added) gained an added pungency during the peak years (1865–1965) of socially sanctioned lynching.

These characteristics were a pollution in the minds and attitudes of those in authority in the Catholic Church who made policies of exclusion the norm of priestly and religious life for African American men and women. These policies of exclusion, and the ease with which they were devised and sustained, have had long-lasting effects, even into our present church. The African American men who chose to offer themselves as prophetic challenges to the prevailing racism of the church regarding priestly and religious vocations were heroic ancestors, no matter the institutional success of their vocational desires. So when we read the words of Thea Bowman (quoted at the beginning of this chapter) that she and her fellow religious, clerical, and lay black Catholics "come to [their] church fully functioning," we must recognize the power of her claim. Within that postulate is a prophetic call to conversion as powerful as that preached by Jonah in the city of Nineveh.

But unlike Nineveh, neither the Catholic Church in the United States nor the culture that so strongly shapes it has undergone appropriate rituals of repentance ("sackcloth and ashes") and reconciliation concerning the sin of racism. Periodic acts of "confession" are beginning steps. Heartfelt (but irregular) commitments of resources on the local and diocesan level are not well grounded, usually, in the institutional structures of power and decision making; and culturally appropriate efforts at vocation recruitment and retention are nonexistent, or minimal at best. While these problems affect all concerned African American Catholics, the crisis within the African American Catholic priesthood is of special concern and worry. The mythic assumptions concerning black men in America are seldom directly addressed, because issues of *race* are seldom directly addressed. Rhetorical warfare is often waged over these issues. Accusations, denials, charges, and countercharges are hurled across cultural and racial chasms. But a *dialogue* that will lead to reconciliation, justice, and community has not been possible in the Catholic Church — or in American society — because the assumptions underlying all analyses and prescriptions concerning race are based in radically different "universes of discourse." When the compelling word of God found Jonah a second time, and the prophet submitted to the divine mandate to preach the forthcoming Day of Judgment, "the people of Nineveh believed God; they proclaimed a fast, and everyone, great and small, put on sackcloth" (Jonah 3:5). When prophetic voices have arisen in the African American Catholic Community — from the times of Daniel Rudd and the Afro-American Lay Catholic Congresses in the late nineteenth century to the frustrated followers of the Reverend George A. Stallings Jr. in the late twentieth century — the most that could be expected were gestures of remorse and amelioration.[34] *Justice* — the presence of right behavior, the restoration of balance to a community, restitution for past inequities — has never been the response.

Several examples gleaned from Stephen Ochs's masterful (and ultimately cautionary) study of the Josephites and their evolving and shifting policies toward the establishment of a black Catholic clergy will be helpful here. Ochs's study, *Desegregating the Altar,* provides the first comprehensive picture of how racism modifies and infects the best "missionary zeal" of those Catholic religious communities whose work is service among African Americans. When he presents the life and thought of the legendary John R. Slattery, first superior general of the Josephites (St. Joseph's Society of the Sacred Heart), Ochs is supremely balanced: he offers Slattery's undaunted courage in demanding a black Catholic clergy and at the same time provides insights into the cultural assumptions of black inferiority and immaturity that

Slattery inherited from his culture and which he never sloughed off, even during his most passionate advocacy. By quoting a letter of Slattery's to Cardinal Herbert Vaughan (the founder of the Mill Hill Fathers, from whom the Josephites are descended), Ochs opens a window on Slattery's perceptions of the "demonization" of black men and then comments on what he sees in that window:

> "[L]ying and fornication are so common... among our best Catholic Negroes, it is no disgrace for an unmarried woman to have a child, and the whiter the bastard, the less the disgrace." Unlike most white Catholics, however, Slattery believed that the church could teach blacks the morality and self-restraint that would keep them from moral degradation. Still doubts persisted. Slattery's rule at St. Joseph's Seminary not to admit any black students under the age of thirty reflected his concern about the ability of virile black males to remain celibate. The issue of black moral capacity would loom larger at the seminary in the year ahead; it was already present at the seminary's inception.[35]

A few years after sending this letter, Slattery proposed to the Josephites that the training of black seminarians be interrupted for one or more years, in order for the men to be under pastoral supervision and scrutiny. The black seminarians would not be allowed to resume their studies without, among other satisfactions of their good standing, a letter written by one of the priests attesting to their "good conduct." As Ochs describes the policy, these rules were made "secret," since they applied only to the black seminarians, "despite Slattery's experience with some rebellious and scandalous white seminarians."[36]

For his time and circumstance, Slattery may be considered as "moderate" or "liberal" in his view concerning "race and culture." His views were more nuanced (relatively) than those of the Catholic bishop of Natchez who flatly opposed black Catholic clergy and for whom "[i]mmorality" loomed as a great problem for the church in its work with Afro-Americans. [Bishop Elder] contended that the moral code of the Catholic church, with its emphasis on the sanctity of marriage and the avoidance of sexual impurity, had no currency among the former slaves. ... The assumption that there was a gulf between the "settled" morality of the church and what they saw as the "unsettled" morality of the freedmen led many white Catholics to regard the freedmen as hopeless semi-barbarians.[37]

Liberalism and moderation, for Slattery and most of the "right-thinking" progressives of that time (including both Booker T. Washington and W. E. B. Du Bois, truth be told), meant cautioning African Americans to be patient and to allow themselves sufficient time to develop the same cultural strengths as were perceived to be the possession of "white" Americans. In commenting on Slattery's policy of delaying entrance to black candidates for the priesthood until their thirtieth year, Ochs remarks that the requirement for white candidates was that they have reached their twentieth birthday. As time progressed, Slattery compromised his sense of gradualism to reflect the concerns of the southern Catholic bishops whose sense of outrage and suspicion guided much of Josephite policy (and the policy of all other orders and congregations serving in the black community) from the 1870s to recent times. In 1894 John Slattery addressed the Fifth Afro-American Lay Catholic Congress and presented his moderate views: "Neither by nature, nor by traditional training can the colored people, taken as a body, stand as yet on the same footing of moral independence as their white brethren."[38]

Since Stephen Ochs utilizes the Josephite archives, the Slattery papers, and the history of the congregation, and since he is writing of the institutional policies governing the treatment of black Catholic candidates for the priesthood, he cannot offer the balance his study cries out for: the story of the men who were considered "arrogant," "immature," "difficult," "unstable," "ungrateful," "troublemakers," and "hostile" — the black candidates themselves; those who departed before their ordination;

and those who lived broken and bitter lives after their ordination. In fact, it seems as if Ochs is occasionally seduced by
his sources, as when he refers to black candidates and priests
as "emotionally unstable." The picture he presents of the institutional grinding away at their self-esteem and maturity might
compel us to use other descriptions, if we could hear from the
men themselves. Other voices, raised by prophetic witnesses in
similar situations, must be added to the accounting. If Slattery,
in some ways the best of the "apostles to the Negroes," could
not confront the hypocrisy of his policies and the flawed subjectivity of his assumptions, how could these black seminarians and
priests survive less enlightened and more blatantly hostile priests,
bishops, and laity wherever they lived and labored? As was asked
before, the question should never be, Why are there so few? but
rather, How can there be *any?*

This aspect of priestly formation and continuance must be
confronted squarely. Since there is little likelihood of the Roman
Catholic Church changing its tradition and structure, the ecclesial community will continue to be organized and controlled by
its clergy. If African American Catholics are considered, even at
the end of the twentieth century, as the recipients of missionary activity; and if African American Catholics are still viewed
by white Catholics and Americans in general (including many
African Americans ourselves) as immature and irresponsible in
the exercise of those qualities deemed essential for successfully
fulfilling the requirements of ordained priesthood, then there will
never be the indigenous church among African Americans that
popes, prophets, and countless "faithful" have demanded for over
one hundred years.

The despair of Jonah is a quality familiar to black Catholic priests, from the time of Augustine Tolton (1854–97) and
Charles Uncles (1891–1933) to the present day. The indictments
and soul-searching laments of Job and Jeremiah have loud echoes
in the *cri de coeur* of *Black Priest, White Church: Catholics and
Racism,* by Lawrence Lucas.[39] In many ways, Lucas's testimony
is a modern version of *David Walker's Appeal,* first published in
1829. Fr. Lucas paints the most vivid picture of the effects of

racism on the soul and mind of the black priest that has ever been committed to print. In thus presenting himself, he fulfills the great warning of the hero of Ralph Ellison's *Invisible Man*:

> When one is invisible he finds such problems as good and evil, honesty and dishonesty, of such shifting shapes that he confuses one with the other, depending upon who happens to be looking through him at the time.... I was never more hated than when I tried to be honest. Or when, even as just now I've tried to articulate exactly what I felt to be the truth. No one was satisfied — not even I. On the other hand, I've never been more loved and appreciated than when I tried to "justify" and affirm someone's mistaken beliefs; or when I've tried to give my friends the incorrect, absurd answers they wished to hear.... I had to take myself by the throat and choke myself until my eyes bulged and my tongue hung out and wagged like the door of an empty house in a high wind.[40]

The irony of such self-mutilating behavior for those African American men who aspire to priesthood and religious commitment within the Roman Catholic Church in the United States rests upon the contradiction inherent in pursuit of a vocation. How can men *choose* voluntary *chastity* in a system where the underlying assumption concerning their existence demands that they be judged as promiscuous, licentious libertines whose cultural flaw concerns sexual impropriety with women and men of all races and ethnic background? Who of them could choose, voluntarily, to live lives of "apostolic poverty," when the culture has made them, from the very beginning of American history, economic commodities to be bartered, sold, or exploited in whatever marketplace prevails at the time? How can men of African descent enthusiastically promise or vow *obedience* to other men who have been taught and conditioned to expect service and subservience from all African American people, who must — by definition — rest at the bottom of all social systems? To choose such restrictions, based as they are on the prevailing myths of racism and oppression that permeate American culture, is to choose a continuous existence of invisibility, impotence, and insanity. Ellison's hero, not surprisingly, speaks to this issue also:

> And my problem was that I always tried to go in everyone's way but my own. I have also been called one thing and then another while no one really wished to hear what I called myself. So after years of trying to adopt the opinions of others I finally rebelled. I am an *invisible* man.[41]

And, yes, the same is true for African American women religious. The emphasis, here, is given to the experience of African American men because the function of priesthood is to be the articulator of the essential truths of faith and community, by which all believers must live. To be a priest, in other words, is to have *words*. If the body of the articulator is suspect, and if the speaker's words are suspect, then what does the exercise of priesthood entail? As Kendall Thomas writes in another (though related) context: "The history of blackness in this country is in large measure a history of degraded bodies and denigrated experience."[42] And that is what most Catholics, no matter their ethnic background, see when they look upon a black man at the altar of God: an *enfleshment* of degradation, denigration, suspicion, and threat. And the throat that opens itself to interpret the word of God and the teachings of the church belongs to an individual who has been all too often rendered mute of his own human, cultural, religious experience, while others have interpreted his existence for him.

Those who would applaud the elevation of certain African American priests to the ranks of the episcopacy; those who seek to include African American men among the procession of the presbyterate; those who believe themselves extraordinarily open and accepting of black men who serve the community at the altar, cannot so express themselves, in this culture, in this church, without, many of them, claiming for themselves an act of virtue. Too often the noblest of sentiments betrays an assumption that many well-intentioned Christians "deserve special credit for being able to treat black people as individuals, as *human beings*," as one cultural critic has stated it.[43]

What are needed, what are desperately sought, by many of the most frustrated and battered women and men who choose the "martyrdom" of priestly and religious life are concerted and collaborative efforts at tearing down the "house that race built" and a communal commitment to establishing a sense of "home" (and *kingdom* and *refuge* and *harbor*).[44] Much like the table set by the Sisters of the Holy Family, written about by Mother Deggs, those who have faced each other across a chasm of denial, oppression, guilt, and shame must be brought to the welcome table.

The issues facing priesthood among African American Catholics are serious and of critical importance to the future of the Black Catholic Church. Leadership is learned, acquired, *and* bestowed upon certain individuals. Even within many black Catholic parishes, African American priests must find strategies for continuous validation of their competence, charism, and legitimacy. Not only has the face of Jesus been wrongly and too-long identified as "Nordic," but the face of leadership within the African American community of Catholics has also been cast in a differing hue from the inhabitants. The same prejudices, stereotypes, and alienating behaviors can be found in any place where "miseducation" has taken root.

The first great antidote to decades of mind poisoning is, of course, the continued presence of those who would commit themselves to the effort of climbing "the rough side of the mountain," of surviving "the belly of the whale," of not only walking the streets of a mythic and mystic Jerusalem but also walking the mean streets of an all-too-real Nineveh. Jonahs keep appearing in our midst, demanding a place at the altar.

In the final pages of this reflection, we shall see what songs need to be sung by such men and women as we have seen appear for our deliverance and for our nourishment. We shall look at what the "hush harbor" of today must do, and listen for the songs that must be sung at the Jericho walls that separate us from real "church." Since we know that we are invited to a banquet, we must be mindful of our best festal behavior.

Chapter Five

Plenty Good Room in the Kingdom

You can talk about me just as much as you please;
I'll talk about you when I get on my knees.

When we sing we announce our existence.

— Bernice Johnson Reagon[1]

If we have taken the image of the circle — the drum — seriously, then we may have admitted a significant shift of consciousness into our meditation. When our thoughts and behaviors reflect the drum, the dance of the "hush harbor" (the ring shout of African American spirituality), instead of the metaphor of evolutionary "progress" — the straight line — we realize that *we don't have to go anywhere* in order to fulfill our destiny, in order to meet God, in order to "join the heavenly band." The *immanence of God* as a concept of African American theology is frequently reflected in the music which speaks of (and to) God with a familiarity and homeliness that have sometimes been attributed to the "child-like" qualities of black people. The sacred purpose of African dancing is to bring God down among and within the people. The mystical union of African American mysticism, dependent on singing and dancing for the act of *transport,* is achieved when the singers and dancers are simultaneously (individually and collectively) at the river, on the earth, down in the valley, up on the mountain, and way up in the middle air. In an analysis of the ring shout, Albert Raboteau offers this pertinent observation:

> In a pattern of overlapping call and response an individual would extemporize the verses, freely interjecting new

ones from other spirituals. Frequently, before he was finished, everyone else would be repeating a chorus familiar
to all. This pattern may be seen as a metaphor for the individual believer's relationship to the community. His [or
her] changing daily experience, like the verses improvised
by the leader, was "based" by the constancy of [the] Christian community. This symbolism is especially powerful in
the ring shout when the individual shouter stood outside
himself, literally in ecstasy, transcending time and place as
the rhythms of the chorus were repeatedly beat out with
hands, feet, and body in the constant shuffle of the ring.[2]

What an apt design for a nourishing and restorative faith-
community Raboteau presents in this description of the ring
shout. This description challenges us to rethink liturgical leadership, individual participation, and responsibilities to the well-
being and strength of the community; it offers a vision of how
one's faith life must be understood as being holistic. The leader,
in this tradition, must be theologically competent and aesthetically and ascetically "well versed" in the complexities of African
American spirituality. The liturgy which centers this spirituality demands full participation and full acceptance of all those
involved. And all who are involved have responsibilities to be
the "base" — the solid rock — from which the rituals are able
to spring into ecstasy and union. The community grounds the
achievement of the individual, while the talent of the individual draws the community to new considerations of itself. Black
sacred songs are the fountain from which this spirituality flows,
from which this model of *church* emerges, from which the theology finds its richness. And, ultimately, the songs, the communal
involvement, and the active, flexible leadership provide an opportunity for every member of the "ring" to do his and her best,
according to the gifts and needs of each.

This is not a vision of a romanticized and idealized future.
Jubilee actually happened. The enslaved set themselves free; the
oppressed and the captive were redeemed. African American
spirituality was one of the means by which a people became

beloved to themselves and found the strength for the freedom journey. The task for those who would desire to go out and invite to the banquet those on the roadside and in the bushes is this: *sankofa* — to return and fetch that which has been lost.

Priestly Leadership

In her masterwork, *Beloved*, Toni Morrison presents a liturgy in a wilderness that can serve as a model for our vision of what an authentically black and truly Catholic sense of ritual might engender among us. The griot figure of this novel, "Baby Suggs, holy," would regularly carry her crippled body into a clearing near the black settlement and preside over a ring shout that has been subtly transformed by Morrison's narrative skills into a sermon and, simultaneously, a vision of the Apocalypse:

> After situating herself on a huge flat-sided rock, Baby Suggs bowed her head and prayed silently. The company watched her from the trees. They knew she was ready when she put her stick down. Then, she shouted, "Let the children come!" And they ran from the trees toward her.[3]

After the children have been commanded to appear in the clearing, the rest of the watching crowd is invited into the circle. First the children are told to laugh. Then the grown men are called forth and told to dance for the women and children. The women are instructed to "cry, for the living and the dead. Just cry." Supremely centered and self-effacing, the presiding holy woman allows the spirit of the assembly to ignite the souls of the participants:

> [A]nd then it got mixed up. Women stopped crying and danced; men sat down and cried; children danced, women laughed, children cried until, exhausted and riven, all and each lay about the Clearing damp and gasping for breath. In the silence that followed, Baby Suggs, holy, offered up to them her great big heart. (88)

Sursum Corda. "Lift up your hearts," the novel tells us. "And love your self," Baby Suggs, holy, crippled, and spirit-filled, exhorts the transported assembly. The sermon Baby Suggs delivers is a combination of hard-won strategies for claiming the self, in the midst of chaos and destruction, and a physical demonstration of transcending one's limitations. She provides a spiritual anatomy lesson, telling her attendees to love their flesh, their skin; their hands, mouths, necks; their "life-holding womb" and their "private parts"; and most of all their hearts, even more than they love their lungs and liver. "Hear me now, love your heart. For this is the prize," she tells them.

> Saying no more, she stood up then and danced with her twisted hip the rest of what her heart had to say while the others opened their mouths and gave her the music. Long notes held until the four-part harmony was perfect enough for their deeply loved flesh. (89)

The ritual of the clearing is a direct gloss on Raboteau's description of the ring shout. The ring shout, the circle dance, is one of the primal African American rituals of power and authority. At the very beginning of this book we explored the meaning of *minkisi*, objects of medicinal healing, invested with the power (*àshe*) to make things happen. It was suggested, then, that the black sacred songs and the stories, proverbs, and artifacts of slavery became such sacred objects for African Americans. Morrison's use of the ring shout in this novel written at the end of the twentieth century demonstrates how the memory of song and dance continues to elicit healing, even when the evocation is a story only to be read. For we who would understand the role of priestly leadership in a church that would be authentically black and truly Catholic, the reality of the ring shout can teach us new ways of looking at the role of the liturgical minister, a role that is rarely understood.

Baby Suggs has gained her authority within the worshiping community because she opens her great heart to their needs and uses her openness to speak on their behalf. She initiates the ritual, even though the assembly has learned to anticipate the event.

They have followed her to the woods, and they await her signal, playfully hiding among the trees until she has determined the correct time for beginning the ceremony.

Her authority is deepened by the fact that she bears the wounds of enslavement. The "power of her office" derives from her experience and her willingness to display her personal history as being representative of the collective history of the assembly. Her first act for the community is one of *discernment*. She calls each group to perform a defining act. Children laugh, men dance, women cry. Baby Suggs, holy, then stretches forth the rhythm, like a master drummer of western Africa. She makes the time stop, so that each group can act out the reality they share with one another. In her most subtle fashion, Morrison presents a picture of a group of people moving from pathology to health when men, women, and children "forget themselves" and become each other, in front of each other, for the re-creation of all. What Baby Suggs maintains within her great overflowing heart, the assembly distinguishes and then blurs. We are all men; we are all women; we are all children. Each of us must weep, dance, and laugh, if we are to be cleansed ("riven") of the terror of our histories.

Baby Suggs is holy because she both absorbs this total reality and dispenses it by orchestrating the community's performance of its possibilities. At first they are in hiding. Then they move silently to the center of the clearing. Next they follow the command of the old woman who has borne and lost children to slavery's demonic furnace. The contagious joy that erupts in the clearing when the several groups share their roles in an ecstatic feast creates a community that changes reality, even as it comes into existence. The incomplete nature of all rituals is underscored by the verbal sermon Baby Suggs delivers, once the laughing, crying, and dancing have ended. "If you are to keep the taste of this moment alive," she seems to say, then you must store up the power you have felt, for the inevitable moment when you are challenged with destruction and annihilation. Morrison introduces one of her enduring themes at this moment in the narrative. The power of the imagination to restore, to heal, to undo tragedy is the theme of this passage, of this novel, of much of the creative work of Morrison. Baby Suggs, we are told, instructs the assembly to become artist-healers: "She told them that the only grace they could have was the grace they could imagine. That if they could not see it, they would not have it" (88). The character of Baby Suggs is constructed to be a "discerner of spirits." She is the one who discerns what healing transformations are needed by each element of the community. Baby Suggs uses her authority, her being seated on the rock, in order to ensure the proper enactment of the rituals, which frees each participant to become *possessed* by the needs and gifts of the others. Her openness to the workings of the spirit she carries within her demonstrates how the people ("the faithful") should be open to one another and to the prompting of the imagination ("the divine"). She has the integrity of the circle as her highest responsibility. As a priest, she teaches; she establishes order; she presides over the communal banquet; and she controls the rituals of healing. Baby Suggs is the exemplar of the most important of the African and African American virtues, *generosity*. The rituals over which she presides, both the banquet and the gathering in the clearing, do not have sufficient power, however, to completely exorcise the great wounding sin of her people: selfishness. Because the pathology of slavery has infected even those who have escaped the physical dangers, none of these rituals is powerful enough to stay the madness that also lurks in the wilderness surrounding the clearing and the people's refuge. When the community has committed the "unforgivable sin" in her eyes — malevolently turning away from impending danger, out of spite and retaliation against the happiness of one if its members — she retreats into her room and there "she used the little energy left her for pondering color" (4).

Through the special quality of her own imagination, Toni Morrison invests the character of Baby Suggs with insights important to us, as we try to "see" the rituals of inclusion and healing needed in the Black Catholic Church. "The grace they could imagine" becomes, for us, an understanding that we choose the symbols by which we organize our self-image and our collective undertakings. African Americans carry within us, every one of us, only one *essential* or "universal" quality of blackness, no matter how many authoritarian voices insist on defining "how to be black." We share the fact of historical enslavement. We do not, all of us, share the same historical responses to this fact of enslavement.

Some of our enslaved ancestors chose, as their first and only response to enslavement, suicide. Others chose murder. Some engaged in infanticide or in self-mutilation as a crude and horrific form of birth control. Some Africans let their minds slip into madness, autism, or depression so severe they were able to remove their feeling from their circumstance.

Some learned the ways of the enslaver and worked psychological juju on their oppressors through subtle resistances and manipulations. Some physically left. If the legends are to be believed, some leapt into the sky and flew back to Africa. Others ingratiated themselves to their oppressors by gossip, brutality, or betrayal and "earned" their "freedom" at the expense of the lives of their fellow enslaved sisters and brothers. Some became "white." For many African American women and men, putting on the "armor" of Christianity helped them endure whatever other choices they saw as possible for them. More than we will ever know rejected all forms of Christianity, some divesting their minds and hearts of all spiritual comforts, others maintaining a link to old ways and old understandings of how to make sense of a senseless world.

The sermon in the clearing pronounced by Baby Suggs, even though it appears in a novel, illustrates the distillation of one set of historical responses to slavery. (Other incidents and situations in *Beloved* illustrate other human ways of dealing with an unspeakable inhumanity.) Those gathered around the rock in the clearing are told to use their imaginations to see a world where they are whole, are valued, are completely at ease, and are joined in a circle of honesty and acceptance. Through the inventory of their gifts, the assembly is told to make an accounting of themselves by which they are rendered of immense value. This fictional sermon has its harmonic link with the words of Thea

Bowman which have grounded much of our study in this text. When Sr. Thea announced that we come to our church fully formed and then listed all the gifts black Catholics bring to the church, she was performing a ritual closely aligned with the one represented by Morrison.

But there is an important difference, beyond the obvious one that one account is fictional and the other is historically factual. Baby Suggs preaches and dances her prophecy to an all-black congregation, with the implied audience of readers possessing a variety of social identities. Thea Bowman uttered her prophetic comments to those (the Roman Catholic bishops of the United States) who would exercise defining power over her black sisters and brothers. In this difference of audiences, we are reminded that *black preaching*, like many other elements of African American culture, must answer to many needs. The "church" of the clearing in *Beloved* is the archetypal symbol of black religious experience in the diaspora. The sermon preached from this rock is a text calling the hearers to contemplate their liberation. The "speech" Sr. Thea gave to the bishops was a *call to conversion* — which is the first step toward *justice*. Beyond that, of course, the texts are more alike than they are different, with one of the most important similarities being in the delivery. Song, gesture, proclamation, exhortation, and admonition are present in both texts. And so is the litany of black giftedness. The symbols Morrison chooses for her created character are symbols of health and holiness. The symbols Bowman selects for her public persona also deal with qualities which are antithetical to all notions of pathology:

> I bring myself, my black self, all that I am, all that I have, all that I hope to become. I bring my whole history, my traditions, my experience, my culture, my African American song and dance and gesture and movement and teaching and preaching and healing and responsibility as gift to the church.[4]

We know from the other sources of information about her life that Thea Bowman used these gifts as the syllabus of her teaching, lecturing, and performing before and among all her various audiences; and her rhetorical style was to make her entire audience *black*, for the duration of her instruction (just as Baby Suggs makes her audience *whole* and *healed* for the time of her preaching and dancing), and to keep each cultural group distinctly aware of its responsibilities to itself and to the others in proximity to it (just as the men and women and children were brought into the fictional circle with their particular circumstances confronted).

Because of the criminalization of African identity and the demonization of black sexuality; because of the political efforts to exploit black experience as evidence of deviance and pathology; because of the "invisibility" of black autonomy and power, it is of vital importance that a message of wholeness and holiness be preached, in season and out of season, to those who have been called "everything but a child of God." In this context, the role of preaching, teaching, and catechesis is to replace one set of images with a new set of symbols. "Anybody ask you who you are, tell them you a child of God," the old folks sang; and we must find a way to sing the same song, in whatever wilderness presents itself. The role of priestly leadership in this context will center upon the initiation of the proper rituals; oversight that the rituals are properly performed; and a complete immersion into the spirituality of liberation, redemption, reconciliation, and healing that can be accomplished only when the people are allowed the time and space to see themselves completely in the rituals.

While there has been a long and compelling history of definitions of blackness having been imposed on people of African descent from within and without the culture, it must nevertheless be said that it is almost always futile to finish the phrase "to be black is..." As was suggested earlier, the historical fact of the enslavement of African peoples is the one essential, universal, shared quality of all who would call themselves *African American* or *Negro* or *colored* or *black*. In matters of African American spirituality, however, certain essential qualities should be contemplated, discussed, or suggested for adoption by those who would engage their minds, souls, and bodies in the worship of God and the reverence of each other in a way that is "authentically black." And these qualities will be found, first and foremost, in the sacred songs and in the rituals that these songs nurture and shape.

How can a community be formed in the midst of chaos or imposed disorder? How can men and women who have been separated from their language groups forge connections to one another for the sake of comfort and protection? How do those who are the victims of abuse and brutality reconstitute themselves into human beings as fully functioning as is possible under the circumstances? How can a dispossessed, degraded, and denigrated people find strategies for psychological stability and for the renewal of hope? These questions have been answered in profound and lasting ways in the exercise of religion among African peoples everywhere in the world. And the exercise of religion, as we have seen over and over in this study, permits some efforts at establishing principles of worship. From these principles, we may imagine a church that is *universal* in its ability to provide a "welcome table" for all who would consider themselves to be dispossessed, devalued, and abandoned: in other words, there is a place for all seekers at the mercy seat of the black church.

Those who would be chosen and set apart to lead and guide the worship of African American Catholic communities must be thoroughly educated in the richness of black sacred song; in the glorious story of black liberation; in the methods of African American asceticism; and in the principal manifestations of African American aesthetics. Issues of inculturation and acculturation may be ultimately distracting, when applied to the development of a church that is authentically black and truly Catholic, if those appointed for service through liturgical ministry are not adequately instructed in the positive, comprehensive components of African American spirituality.

Old-time Religion

Our education begins with the music created by those for whom literacy was a death sentence; music that appropriated multiple drum rhythms into songs and sermons that possessed multiple levels of understanding and comprehension; music that engaged mind, heart, soul, and body in its performance and appreciation.

Music such as this becomes the second universally shared quality of African American experience. The music helped generate, quite often, the inner resources with which enslaved Africans resisted the most dehumanizing elements of slavery and by which they were able to link themselves together into an often "invisible" community. Wyatt Tee Walker bestows high praise on black sacred music:

> The music of the Black religious tradition can be a vital instrument for a ministry of social change.... The music ...operates on two levels: first, psychologically and emotionally — it locates the people's sense of heritage, their roots, where they are and where they want to go; and secondly, it mobilizes and strengthens the resolve for struggle. A people's sense of destiny is rooted in their sense of history. Black sacred music is the primary reservoir of the Black people's historical context and an important factor in the process of social change.[5]

In the music is found the genealogy of the "faith family" reconstructed to replace the family histories destroyed by the Middle Passage. The music served as schoolroom, newspaper, courtroom, and village square. Black sacred song has been used as coded communications for the passengers and conductors of the Underground Railroad. When the oldest songs are no longer accessible to an increasingly large number of African Americans, the circle of culture becomes fractured anew, and many of the qualities that Wyatt Walker and others attribute to the music are not available for a new generation of African Americans who are undergoing new forms of old horrors. The people who exhorted each other to "steal away" to the bush/hush harbor because they knew that they had "been in the storm so long" were seeking "a rock in a weary land," where they could be given a "little time to pray." When they stepped into their counterclockwise circle, became the "band all dressed in white/red," and reenacted the great battle of Jericho, or felt themselves delivered like "Daniel from the lions' den," they were making themselves available to receive the power of God. And this power was not just to claim a seat in the kingdom, but to find physical energy and spiritual composure with which to withstand one more day of exile and orphanage. Bernice Johnson Reagon teaches us to value the power of the music when she encourages congregational singing as a way of social transformation: "Songs are a way to get to singing, though singing is what you're aiming for. And the singing is running sound through your body. You cannot sing a song and not change your condition."[6] At this point in her conversation, Reagon is discussing the physiological implications of singing. In other words, how does the *physics* of singing work? From our study of western African dancing and the autohypnotic qualities of trance singing, we can better appreciate her insights. When we sing, we change our pulse, heartbeat, muscular tension, and posture. That physical change allows our emotions and senses to change also. Reagon goes on to say:

> I am talking about a culture that thinks it is important to exercise this part of your being. The part of your being that is tampered with when you run this sound through your body is a part of you that our culture thinks should be developed and cultivated, and that you should be familiar with, that you should be able to get to as often as possible, and that if it is not developed, you are underdeveloped as a human being. If you go through your life and you don't meet this part of yourself, somehow the culture has failed you.[7]

Bernice Reagon shares, in her stories of growing to adulthood in Georgia, how she did not consciously have to learn the traditional songs of black culture. They were as familiar to her as the air she breathed. During her college years she became a member of the Student Non-violent Coordinating Committee and was one of the founders of the "Freedom Singers" of SNCC. Traveling throughout the United States, organizing communities, participating in voter registration projects, leading rallies, being threatened and thrown in jail, Reagon and hundreds of her fellow "freedom warriors" depended on the old songs of slavery to sustain them for the resurrected terrors of the 1960s. So it is something other than the predictable dyspepsia of the disapproving elder that leads her to worry about the disconnection of the culture from the songs she learned to sing at the very "gates of hell": "I felt like there was no air I breathed that these songs didn't exist in. They are not being passed today in the same way. I'm not sure if black people can get through the next century without this repertoire."[8]

In fact, Reagon clearly states that some music of the young will always be concerned with telling the truth of their existence. Her strong caution is reserved (across all social categories) for any examples of abuse toward women and children, acts of violence and brutality, and intervention against any human beings, be they individuals or nations. As she says, the only requirement for a freedom song is that it be concerned with the liberation of all.

In her discussion of spirit-possession, Bernice Reagon suggests a reason why many African Americans (and other Americans, in general) are not learning the traditional songs as previous generations learned them, like the air they breathed. Using the song "This Little Light of Mine" as her reference, Reagon spells out the difference between some Baptist churches and the rise of Pentecostal denominations. In her analysis of spirit-possession, she says: "Possession came into the service through the sermon.... [I]n Pentecostal churches the Spirit is accessible to anybody at any point [that] the rhythms and the energy and the spirit would be there." One ritual is dominated by the preacher (the cleric) in charge. The other is "free" in its expectations that the fire of the Holy Spirit will touch wheresoever it will. When Baptist and Methodist conventions demanded more and more control of the services through a growing dependence on literacy (as a requisite for ordination and as a method of congregational singing), many disaffected congregants left the increasingly "mainstream" churches and sought spaces where they and the Holy Spirit were untrammeled. This movement to Pentecostal and "holiness" churches also had within it a rejection of the rampant sexism that was growing more and more stifling in the Baptist and Methodist denominations. A third element was a growing uneasiness in these churches for the seemingly retrogressive ways of rural blacks, as opposed to the more "civilized" ways of acculturated urban Negroes.

Mainly for these reasons the phenomenon of spirit-possession came under relentless attack. Every effort was made to bring all aspects of worship under the control of the pastor/preacher. Bernice Reagon displays much wit and scholarship when she goes on to comment:

> In Pentecostal churches, it's open season.... Operating at full power and inviting people in the congregation to operate at full power is a very important Africanism within the society — not being afraid of a room of very powerful people... and actually stimulating people to operate at full power.[9]

The declension of power seems simple enough. In the Pentecostal tradition, the music and the preaching have equal importance. All those assembled are open to the sound "running through their bodies," and they make themselves available to possession by the Spirit of God. Upon receiving the fire of the Spirit, the faithful are given all the spiritual gifts outlined by St. Paul in 1 Corinthians 12 (apostleship; prophecy; teaching; speaking in tongues; etc.). When the fullness of Pentecost has hit a church, the result is very much akin to a communal celebration in the most traditional of religious observances in western Africa — or elsewhere in the African diaspora. When the Spirit takes possession of a believer, "a saint," the one so captured is as "fully formed" as any could hope to be.

It is not surprising, first, that few ministers in charge of congregations would encourage such a "taking away" of power (authority) in the church; and, second, that such a widespread outpouring of the Holy Spirit is virtually impossible in most sites of Roman Catholic worship. (Part of the popular understanding of being "Catholic" must surely reside in "being book-dependent for all liturgical behavior.") From such reflections we may more easily understand just how unnerving black sacred song (traditional or more contemporary) would be if incorporated into most Roman Catholic liturgies. Returning once again to Sr. Thea Bowman's 1989 address to the Catholic bishops, we will find her in strong agreement with Bernice Reagon's understanding of the power of a community of believers "fully alive." Even before announcing that black people are abundantly, prodigally gifted, Sr. Thea slips into a bit of signifying, when she sets up a rhetorical trap: "What does it mean to be black and Catholic? It means that I come to my church fully functioning. *That doesn't frighten you, does it?*"[10] Lest any of her listeners slip out of the trap, Sr. Thea returns several times to those very issues that would (and do) frighten "ministers in charge," no matter their denomination. Her tossed-aside definition of *multiculturalism* is much to the point here: "See, you all talk about what you have to do if you want to be a multicultural church: Sometimes I do things your way; sometimes you do things mine" (35).

In a comment that does not appear in the printed version of her address (quoted here from the filmed presentation), she reminds the bishops that their documents on racism, especially *Brothers and Sisters to Us*, have gone largely unread, even unnoticed. Sr. Thea demonstrates her prophetic gift when she brings into the open the resistance of many black Catholics to all notions of cultural renewal within the Black Catholic Church. Echoing the comments we have read from Joseph Davis concerning "extraordinary ministry," she decries the "missionary mentality" of many black Catholics and pinpoints the resistance to introducing African American elements of worship to Catholic liturgical expression: "Some black people don't approve of black religious expression in Catholic liturgy. They've been told that it's not properly Catholic. They've been told that it's not appropriately serious or dignified or solemn or controlled, that the European way is necessarily the better way" (35). Who are the "they" who have been miseducating these black Catholics? Sr. Thea is far too polite to point a finger at any in her audience. But someone in authority must bear the responsibility.

Since she ends her address with a firm admonition that the bishops devote more of their time, energy, and material resources to increasing opportunities for the education of black people, it is clear that Sr. Thea's theme is to use her own life as an example of how black Catholic leadership is developed. Because she was offered a better education through the Catholic school of Canton, Mississippi, than she would have received from the public school system, she was drawn to join both the church and the religious community which staffed the school. She wants the same opportunity for many others.

And she knows that ignorance is the death of her people, and the death of her church. But the ignorance will not be dispelled by the advantage of classroom education. If black people are to be fully functioning adult Catholics, the education must entail a thorough grounding in the gifts they bring to the church universal. Thea Bowman knows very well that what looks like a gift to her may appear to be a defect in the eyes of others (including the eyes of some in her episcopal audience):

> They still talk about black folk in the church. You hear it, you know, you hear it over on the sidelines. They say we're lazy. They say we're loud. They say we're irresponsible. They say we lower the standards. So often we've been denied the opportunities to learn and to practice. You learned by trial and error; ain't that how you learned? And to grow. (35)

The connection she makes to these "they" statements and to the bishops assembled before her is painfully obvious to read and to watch. Her not-so-gentle indictment of the absence of black participation in the "normal, church-authorized consultative processes that attempt to enable the people of God to be about the work of the Catholic Church" (34) includes her pointing out that in some cases even black bishops are not included in these processes. The inherited prejudice of white leadership can be transformed into *racism* by the easy inattentiveness to the *invisibility of black people* in positions of authority throughout the institutional offices of the Catholic Church. "See, you all

talk about what you have to do if you want to be a multicultural church: Sometimes I do things your way; sometimes you
do things mine." How is that possible if there is no one black
present to suggest a different way of doing things?

These reflections by Thea Bowman are connected to the picture of Pentecostalism painted by Bernice Johnson Reagon. The
"business" of being Catholic means being quiet, being dignified,
being (self-)controlled, being subservient, and being deferential
to appointed authority. Any behavior to the contrary would fall
under the description of black people that Sr. Thea once again
attributes to the wicked "they":

> How can we teach all the people what it means to be black
> and Catholic? The *National Catechetical Directory* says that
> all catechesis is supposed to be multi-cultural, but how little
> of it is. When we attempt to bring our black gifts to the
> church, people who do not know us say we're being non-
> Catholic or separatists — or just plain uncouth. (35)

"People who do not know us" must include those black Catholics mentioned earlier, the ones who are suspicious or adversarial
to the introduction of black cultural traditions into "Catholic"
worship. It should be evident by now that what would be introduced, what Sr. Thea and Bernice Reagon (and others) would
call "black gifts," entails more than energetic music and enthusiastic prayer. The "gifts of black folk," beginning with black
sacred song, would inevitably introduce a reordering of the authority structure of the church and would inevitably demand a
sharing of power dependent on the gifts of the Holy Spirit as
much as being dependent on the acquisition of formal education
credentials.

> I got shoes, you got shoes, all God's children got shoes.

> This little light of mine, I'm going to let it shine,
> let it shine, let it shine, let it shine.

In order for the claim of inheritance to be made effectively,
those who feel themselves to be "motherless [children] a long

way from home" (in the words of the song Sr. Thea sang to the bishops) must, like Sr. Thea herself, learn to let the power of the old songs course through their bodies and their souls. Bernice Reagon says it well when she admits that many young people nowadays reject the old songs because they do not know the stories that should wrap each song in meaning. Building on Reagon's insights, we learn that, for someone to sing "I got shoes, you got shoes," the listeners must know what the singer *means*. And the meaning of the song will shift, depending on the concrete and specific meanings locked in the particular experience of the singer at *each* singing of the song. At one time, "shoes" could mean "spiritual gifts." At another time, "shoes" could mean "stolen property" or "a place in the kingdom of God" or even "a pair of shoes," after a lifetime of material deprivation. So stories must accompany the songs, and the songs must illustrate and magnify the stories. More and more, prophetic witnesses must be raised by the Spirit and by the needs of the community to emerge from the invisibility of the shadows, to face the inherent risks in singing songs that will be disruptive of good order and dignified services. Testimony must be given because the minute song replaces silence, all who are touched by the performance are transformed. In a passage very much to the point of these observations, the poet Audre Lorde makes this declaration:

> And of course I am afraid, because the transformation of silence into language and action is an act of self-revelation, and that is always fraught with danger.... In the cause of silence, each of us draws the face of her own fear — fear of contempt, of censure, or some judgment, or recognition, of challenge, of annihilation. But most of all, I think, we fear the visibility without which we cannot truly live.[11]

Meeting at the Building

All participants in the ring shout, those dancing in the center of the circle, those forming the circle, those sitting or standing on the outside, providing the rhythmic support and "base," invest their total selves in the ritual, and all expect to receive the benefit of the sacred act: the power of God's Spirit raining down upon them. This understanding of liturgical involvement is invoked, universally, when competent liturgical theologians discuss the role of liturgy in the lives of Christians. Nothing, we are told, is more central to the life of faith than the liturgy of the church. The great renewal of the liturgy that gained impetus with the documents of the Second Vatican Council has had as profound an impact on the lives of Catholic Christians and other denominations as any single event in the renewal of Christian life in the twentieth century. And that is as it should be, for we are told:

> [T]he liturgy is the summit toward which the activity of the Church is directed; at the same time it is the fountain from which all her power flows.... The liturgy in turn inspires the faithful to become "of one heart in love" when they have tasted to their full of the paschal mysteries; it prays that "they may grasp by deed what they hold by creed.... From the liturgy, ... especially from the Eucharist, as from a fountain, grace is channeled into us; and the sanctification of [all] in Christ and the glorification of God, to which other activities of the Church are directed as toward their goal, are most powerfully achieved.[12]

What draws us to the welcome table, what takes place while we are gathered in that sacred circle, and what we carry with us as we return to the large world outside the "clearing" define us as pilgrim travelers on the highway to heaven. But the Eucharist, we have been told, must be worthily offered:

> But in order that the sacred liturgy may produce its full effect, it is necessary that the faithful come to it with proper dispositions, that their thoughts match their words, that they cooperate with divine grace lest they receive it in vain.... Pastors of souls must therefore realize that, when the liturgy is celebrated, more is required than the mere observance of the laws governing valid and licit celebra-

tion. It is their duty also to ensure that the faithful take part knowingly, actively, and fruitfully.[13]

In the best of all possible worlds, this injunction, simply stated, would be, in itself, commentary enough on the proper method of liturgical development in the Black Catholic Church. Therefore, some further comment seems appropriate.

The faithful must take part *knowingly*, *actively*, and *fruitfully*. For there to be a wide flowering of African American liturgical practice in the Catholic Church in the United States, the "welcome table" will have to be established on the "rock" of the old-time religion we have been studying in this book. This is not to say that there is only *one* way of presenting authentic African American worship. As Clarence Joseph Rivers instructed us decades ago:

> Whereas some blacks will unrightfully object to the introduction of black culture out of self-hatred; still other blacks may very rightfully object to the introduction of only one facet of black culture as if that single facet were the whole jewel. While wanting to be their black selves, blacks will not want to have themselves described and defined in any way which will limit their freedom.[14]

There is plenty good room in the kingdom and as many ways of praising God as there are rooms in the mansions of God. One of the strengths of the liturgical renewal sparked by Fr. Rivers in the 1960s and 1970s (and carried on by dozens of others since then) is the wide variety of authentic worship experiences that have nourished faith-communities throughout the United States and that have provided grace and encouragement for many of our sisters and brothers in other denominations and from various ethnic backgrounds. The obligation of those who would continue to guide the renewal of the liturgy in African American Catholic settings is to remember the caution of Rivers. All the facets of black cultural worship must be present in "authentic" black worship.

Just as there is no "right" way to sing the songs known as Negro spirituals, there is no one way to be "black" in church. Artists such as Marian Anderson, Roland Hayes, Paul Robeson, and Jessye Norman, classically trained and devoted to the reclamation of black sacred song, presented the old songs with a measure of artistic genius that set standards for the entire world. But, then, so did the performances of, among others, Mahalia Jackson, the Fairfield Four, Marion Williams, and Rosetta Tharpe. These "traditional gospel" singers established performance styles which are a part of African American religious heritage and must be reverenced by the same congregations that are nourished by the music of the Winans family, Kirk Franklin, Bobby Jones, the Clark Sisters, or whoever has gained popularity at the present time. In addition, the liturgical life of African American Catholics somewhere celebrates such music as that of Gregorian chants and the melodies of Bach, Mozart, and Handel and the modern contributions of composers and singers such as the St. Louis Jesuits and the Monks of Weston Priory.[15] There should be moments available for the most spontaneous, heartfelt affirmations of the Spirit, as well as privileged time and space for the silent absorption of the grace of the event. For us, and for all time, *Catholic* must mean *inclusive*.

However, having made a judicious claim for an inclusive and joyous appropriation of all good liturgical music from everywhere in the world — and demanding that appropriate reverence be paid to the spiritualities that this music will bring to us — I must clearly state my belief that the traditional, "ancestral" music of the black church be given a place of privilege in *all* the worship services, eucharistic and noneucharistic, that engage the faithful assembled in black Catholic churches in the United States. The knowledgeable, active, and fruitful participation of the faithful in effective liturgies in the black Catholic churches admits no abbreviated, discounted process. J-Glenn Murray, S.J., another influential presence in the world of black Catholic liturgical development, says it simply and powerfully: "Our culture may have forgotten permanence, those realities that are eternal, but we have been given a gift of memory. At liturgy and in

sacraments, we remember that our God is slow to anger, rich
in mercy, abounding in steadfast love. God's love never fails."[16]
Unfortunately, Murray's evocation of the "memory of the eternal" finds little support in the actual practices of many liturgists
in the African American Catholic faith-communities. What is
still too often missing is the knowledge of our past, the knowledge of how the spirituality of the ancestors has been kept alive
through the songs and rituals of a (still) "invisible institution" —
slave religion. Because those pastors in whose hands rests the
responsibility for the celebration of effective liturgy, and who
are primarily responsible for the education of the laity (without
which there will be little fruitful participation), do not themselves know the richness of African American spirituality, only
surface adaptations of the liturgy are possible. And such half-
hearted attempts at "acculturation" are doomed to failure and
bound to cause conflict, strife, and resistance. Clarence Joseph
Rivers sounded the warning early in his career, and his message needs periodic reacquaintance. At the beginning of *Soulfull
Worship*, Rivers lists several problems facing those who would attempt to "blend Afro-American culture with Catholic worship:
white racism; black self-hatred; stereotyping; incompetence." Of
most interest to our present discussion are his thoughts on
incompetence:

> A final obstacle to the blending of Catholic worship with
> black culture may be the lack of competence on the part
> of Catholics in certain art forms from the traditional black
> Church. This lack of competence in rather sophisticated
> skills can result in caricature of the black Church tradi-
> tions and make of them something to be smiled at rather
> than admired. . . . [W]hen we perform something poorly
> then we give people an excuse for saying "We don't want
> any part of that. It's no good." On the contrary whatever is
> done should be done so well that people who would want
> to reject it will be moved in spite of themselves and will
> find themselves taken up by it.[17]

All too often pastors (of every ethnic background, including African American) who are not educated in the rich spirituality of black sacred song, gesture, and preaching will be passive participants in mediocrity, allowing equally unschooled musicians and volunteers to impose what is stereotypically "black" upon a seemingly passive congregation which nevertheless resists in just the ways Rivers suggests. "But we have a gospel choir," it will be said. "But we have hired the best musicians, and spent money on the latest recordings and visited some of the liveliest churches in the city," it will be argued. "And nothing seems to please the congregation." The bolder critics will claim that "all that blackness is anti-Catholic," and so on. Sunday liturgies will become hostage — either to the "traditional" crowd or to the "gospel" or "Afrocentric" crowd. While the devil may be the "father of lies," some other demons are the "parents of stubbornness," because many African American churches have rifts within the community, based on a chasm of ignorance into which all sides are prone to stumble. The sacred circle is fractured into shards of hostility and bitter feelings.

"Gospel" radio stations in most urban areas of the United States are not adequate sources of instruction in liturgical theology and appropriate ritual music — not for most black churches, no matter the denomination. The desire to attract young people to our churches cannot be the prevailing impetus for the hiring of ministers of music or for the development of liturgical catechesis and training. As J-Glenn Murray says, "We have been given a gift of memory." With that gift comes the responsibility to teach what the old folks knew and to hand on the lessons of liberation, inclusion, and spiritual confirmation found in a wide variety of rhythms and sentiments. No artist, no matter the medium, can ever master the craft without a thorough appreciation of the great examples of the art being studied. The same is true of African American worship.

Great preaching in the African American tradition admits the example of Henry Mitchell and Ella Pearson Mitchell, Martin Luther King (Sr., Jr., and III), Marian Wright Edelman, Thea Bowman, Howard Thurman, and Sojourner Truth. Not all of these examples (and thousands of other great deliverers of the word) are respected and revered for their enthusiastic, "Pentecostal" style of preaching. What they, and all great black preachers, are known for is the ability to so let the light of their passion shine through their delivery that (as Bernice Reagon observed) the Spirit can take possession of the hearers. That intensity of inspiration may cause one preacher to dance, another to shout, and yet another to pause and catch the tears before they fall from her eyes. That prophetic fire may ignite the entire church in a circus of leaping frenzy and volatile singing and shouting. Or it may call forth the deepest silence imaginable. There is no one way of being black.

The pastors, the ministers of music, the liturgy directors of African American Catholic churches have an obligation to be *catholic* in the breadth of their education in the many traditions of black *theologies;* and they have an equally important obligation to be able to sing, dance, and make themselves available to the claim of the Holy Spirit. If the ministers themselves are afraid of appearing undignified, improper, not serious, or "just plain uncouth," then their sense of inculturation needs a major adjustment — or even a relocation of their ministry. Within black Catholic churches the need for multicultural catechesis means that the liturgies must go as far back as possible in the history of black faith and that the liturgies must re-create the sacred circle in every single liturgical moment. To be authentically black and truly Catholic demands nothing less than such a thorough commitment to accepting African American spirituality as a valid starting point for effective liturgy.

The great danger in employing stereotypical understandings of black culture in the Catholic liturgies is adhering to a belief that *black* and *Catholic* are not already in harmony (indeed, they are sometimes even identical); one result of this misunderstanding is that we may find ourselves subscribing to the conviction that all black churches are Pentecostal in their ritual expressions. Ignorance has never solved a problem. Choir directors and ministers of music who are trained in non-Catholic traditions may inadvertently exacerbate the problem by applying what is comfortable and familiar to them in the absence of clear directives from the pastors and other administrators who are equally deficient in the "stories that cushion the old songs," as Bernice Reagon described the best of black liturgical practice.

The issues being challenged here are rooted in an *ahistorical* impulse concerning liturgy. What is popular, what is current, what is seductive may not be (and most probably is not) most conducive for effective liturgy. In the African American tradition invoked here, the elements of good liturgy are not mainly concerned with what music is being sung at any given service. The main concern here is whether or not the sacred circle is being honored in each event. The circle consists of the holy *ancestors*, the *elders*, the *young*, and those *who labor* in the heat of the sun. No eucharistic liturgy focuses on the present, only; no meaningful prayer service — be it the Liturgy of the Hours or an anointing of children during Lent — can concern itself with only one group from among the whole assembly.

Elders must bless the young. The young must call forth the gifts of the Spirit from within the hearts of the very old. Those who labor for the sake of the family, the community, and the world must receive the thanks of their elders and the respect of the children entrusted to their care. Ministers must be anointed for strength in their service. Teachers must be given a little time to rest awhile, away from the restless urgency of their daily environments. Old stories must be given to those who are desperate to understand a forbidding and daunting world that is not of their making. Underlying this vision of liturgy is a presupposition that black theology is *performance theology*. Such a theology demands that sufficient rituals be employed to provide opportunities for communal needs: witness services, testimonies, confirmation, anointing, mission (or "sending") services, exhortations, reconciliations.

When these tasks are undertaken, the songs and prayers and gestures and rituals of the entire family of God will be available for that portion of the family gathered in prayer. The requirement of Vatican II's Constitution on the Sacred Liturgy will be met. The resultant liturgy will be based on knowledge and not intuition; will engage the entire assembly and not be a showcase for virtuoso performances by the trained ministers only; and will be fruitful — will strengthen those present, honor those who have departed the assembly, and bring into the circle those who are seeking the consolations of faith. Silence will be as valued as the loudest song of praise.

Those African American Catholic communities who are striving to achieve these goals succeed more often than not; and their success usually depends on listening to the spirit of the community and offering simple, effective responses to the needs of the people. These responses are based on solid knowledge and not on the ingestion of fads. Also, a necessary tension is maintained in these communities between creating new and powerful responses to the needs of the people and establishing true rituals. A sense of *performance* theology does not justify a frantic effort to create something new for each gathering, to restructure every liturgy, to adapt the great liturgies of the church, over and over, in a quest to make the liturgies "relevant." Such manic efforts can only cause a deep dissatisfaction among all concerned. Rituals offer comfort by their very predictability, after all. We yearn for the familiar as part of the process of reverencing our cultural memory and as a way of restoring our sense of who we are as a people.

Wishing to be "authentically black" and seeking to reverence the African roots of African American worship, we are brought to an understanding that black cultures maintain their vitality by honoring the old and valuing the traditional. African Americans have inherited the richness of multiple cultures and also some of the infections of those same cultures. Improvisation must always be balanced with a studied understanding of the structure of rituals. Spirit-possessed enthusiastic displays must always be linked with the deeply contemplative, receptive position of "Speak Lord, your servant listens." As one of the recurring verses of the spirituals says, "When I get to heaven, gonna sing and shout / be nobody there to turn me out." When we develop rituals that bring some of heaven into our midst, there will be an appreciation for all the ways people dance, sing, shout, moan, laugh, weep, and sit humbly with their God. And nobody will be turned away from the fountain.

Walk Together, Children; Don't You Get Weary

We ... chosen from among you to serve the People of God, are a significant sign among many other signs that the Black Catholic Community in the American Church has now come of age. We write to you as brothers that "you may share life with us." We write also to all those who by their faith make up the People of God in the United States that "our joy may be complete."

—What We Have Seen and Heard

We love our bishops, you-all. We love you-all too. But, see, these bishops are our own, ordained for the church universal, ordained for the service of God's people, but they are ours. We raised them. They came from our community and in a unique way they can speak for us and to us. ...Indigenous leadership. The leaders are supposed to look like their folks, ain't that what the church say?

— Sr. Thea Bowman

Who will ever know the prayers locked deep in the hearts of the slaves owned by the Maryland Jesuits, or in the hearts of those owned by the Sisters of Charity or the various bishops and prominent Catholic leaders of Louisiana and Georgia and Alabama? Who will ever know if these faithful men and women looked at their sons and prayed that they or their children or grandchildren might — through some miracle of God — be raised up to the altar and be ordained a priest of the church? How many suffering mothers and fathers prayed that some angel might deliver their daughters into a place of refuge and sanctuary behind convent walls where their virtue and goodness might be protected and placed in service for the people who cried out in the wilderness of slavery?

Generations of prayers went before the ordination of Augustus Tolton or the consecration of Henriette de Lille and the other early pioneers of religious life. Bands of prayer were forged for the perseverance of such gifts as Harold Perry and Thea Bowman, Booker Ashe, August Thompson, Francesca Thompson, and all their fellow seekers. All the nuns, priests, seminarians, and postulants who stayed briefly or for a lifetime in formal service to the church were lifted up every day in prayer. And so it goes today. But for whom and what have we prayed all these decades, generations, centuries? In 1984, the black bishops of the United States declared that the Black Catholic Church had reached adulthood. In their pastoral letter, these bishops announced to the world that it was time for black Catholics to become evangelizers to ourselves. And what has been the result?

Throughout the writing of this text the terms "black" and "African American" have been used with great variety of context, much the way the terms are used in normal cultural speech. All cultural signifiers carry great connotative resonance, and this is especially true for the designations by which people of African descent are known and by which they recognize themselves. While a full linguistic meditation on these terms is not possible here, we must at least attend to the fact that negative inheritances also accompany these terms. When the people of "Africa in diaspora" claim an *African American* identity, many permutations of self-disclosure take place. There are "good things" and "bad things" about African cultures and European cultures and American cultures, and those who have been born into these cultural families inherit many more cultural traits than it is usually expedient to admit. The same is true for the multicultural accretions associated with the terms "black Catholic" and "African American Catholic." We are still in a historical flux where those so identified are often much more "Catholic" than "black"; much more "American" than "African." This is one of the reasons that the prophetic call of the black bishops, the visionary writings of Clarence Rivers, and the two-edged preaching of Thea Bowman have been so important to contemporary black Catholic thinking and have served as the foundation for the present study.

If the Black Catholic Church is to present itself in its adulthood; if African American Catholic leadership is to be present in authentic multicultural endeavors ("sometimes I do things your way; sometimes you do things my way"); if liturgy is to ever be "authentically black and truly Catholic," then black Catholics must serve *new wine in new wineskins* at the welcome table that we prepare as a sign that the kingdom is among us. The gifts by which we have been gifted must be gathered and displayed in ways that give honor to those who first sang and prayed us into existence — those whose lives and endeavors endowed the church we now claim — and honor to those whose sacrificed lives were seeds of glory broadcast in an often cruel and hostile church.

The sorriest and most ignominious of the heirlooms of our "creolized"[18] existence are presenting ominous challenges to our growth and flowering. The traditional black virtues of *generosity* and *hospitality* are frequently choked by "American values" of individualism, selfishness, suspicion, and jealousy. In many African American settings the tradition of honoring the elders and showing reverence for the ancestors has been all but strangled by the "contemporary" and "modern" disposition to be addicted to all things new and immediate. A "people with a memory" have become a group of individuals who do not know their own history. Too many of us spend much of our spiritual endowment looking over our shoulders lest outsiders see us act our true selves and find us somehow lacking. The culture of the gun and the lynching ritual as the final arbiters of rude justice, promulgated by centuries of American mythology concerning the conquering of an ever-shifting frontier by rugged and (heavily armed) individualists, has permeated the black community like an airborne virus.[19] Even those critics who would caution African Americans against romanticizing the past with a false nostalgia (a decidedly *American* tendency) for "good old days that never were" will admit that the escalating importation of drugs into the African American population (with the violence and destruction which are its companion plagues) has qualitatively changed the nature of black life in the United States.

The Black Catholic Church has been called to adult responsibilities in a time of apocalyptic upheavals. In order to respond to this unique opportunity to become a light, set upon a stand for all to see, the Black Catholic Church must divest itself of what seems antithetical to the traditions of cultural healing and transformation that are the best of being *black;* it must lay down "by the riverside" those attributes of a mission church which no longer work within the black community (and which seem not to be working for many other segments of the Catholic community). First and of the highest priority, the education and formation of priests and religious must be culturally based and economically supported within the African American Catholic community.

A church come of age must steward its own institutions, offering guidance, financial support, and political and institutional protection, whenever possible and wherever necessary. In the area of seminary training, the African American Church has reached a plateau from which it can be "educators of itself." The hundreds of supremely gifted African American scholars, lay, religious, and clerical, whose intellectual gifts are sought by the finest colleges, universities, and educational foundations can be brought together in a variety of more effective ways for the training of clergy and religious who would be "authentically black and truly Catholic," instead of being educated, most often, with the goal of proving that the old demonizations of black men and women are not true, most often by becoming *exceptions* to whatever stereotype may prevail. The great effort to send African American men and women into seminaries, monasteries, and convents has been historically directed as much at the goal of validating the religious gifts of black Catholics as at supplying indigenous workers in the African vineyards. Surviving the system was (and still is) the highest goal to which many of these men and women could aspire. And it was enough, for many black Catholics, to know that Father (or Brother or Sister) was persevering as a role model — not necessarily to younger black women and men but to the nonblack community that surrounded them. The apostolic ministry for many priests and religious was presenting themselves to the larger, white church as being worthy of inclusion.

The ironic truth of this assertion can be found in the memoirs and historical anecdotes of countless black priests, brothers and sisters who were held under the deepest suspicion during their formative years in church institutions and who then experienced significant rejection and hostility from black Catholics, often of a more virulent strain than what they experienced in nonblack communities. If Father (or Brother or Sister) survived the training, the likelihood was that these survivors would be tolerated — or even absorbed — in places where they would be viewed as examples of tolerance and transformation. In black Catholic communities, the response could sometimes be (and in some places still is) much more problematic. Some ordained and vowed African Americans have been met with the feasting for the "child come home." Others have been met with deep-rooted rejection because they did not wear the face of legitimate ecclesial authority or speak with the tones of a "valid" representative of Christ. Many of the reasons for these reactions have already been discussed, one way or another, in the course of this study. What needs attention here is the opportunity to build anew on the solid ground of a positive black theology.

Priestly and religious vocations emerge from the prayers of the community, and those who are called to such apostolic service should be trained, first, as caretakers of the cultural and spiritual gifts of their people. Why? So that they can be protectors of the sacred circle. They should be trained to know that every apostolic act must be an effort at strengthening each member of the circle (elders, the young, those who labor in the heat of the sun); that preaching, teaching, sanctification, and healing may often entail providing time, space, protection, and advocacy for all the otherwise invisible and neglected members of their communities. In an age when old ways of community preservation and protection must be rediscovered, and new ways of liberation and holiness must be made available in times of crisis, there must be an increasing number of formally appointed ecclesiastical leaders who have been tested and approved *by their own communities* because they possess those gifts most needed by the community, as the community itself perceives those needs.

Communities can be guided through discernment more effectively and gracefully than by edict, task force, or position paper. The awakening in the community of the gifts of freedom, profound love of scripture, contemplation, joy, spirituality, and reconciliation that are spoken of in *What We Have Seen and Heard* means having leadership trained to see these gifts as of the highest value for the survival of African American communities, churched and unchurched. Clerical and episcopal leadership has a special obligation to invite to the table women and men of great giftedness who can oversee, administer, sponsor, monitor, and dream into reality the programs and structures that will be the most effective tools for the rebuilding of black churches as both holy sanctuary and cities of refuge. And these clerical and episcopal leaders will not rise to the task set before them by the long line of holy men and women who constitute the circle of our blackness unless they are willing to "dance in the midst of the circle" themselves.

It was traditional throughout much of the rural black South for the elders of a family to remind children, as they were leaving their homes, "When you go out there, you remember where you came from." Do not bring shame to the home of your ancestors. That injunction has not been lost in these more modern times. It was one of Thea Bowman's self-appointed tasks to remind many black priests (and a few black bishops) that their "folks" were keeping a watchful eye upon them, and they should remember where they came from, "who their people were." It is a part of the traditional concept of "black family love." To be such a leader is to embody the best of the cultural and spiritual values of the people being led and to demonstrate in one's person how those gifts and values can be constantly renewed and appropriated for the needs of the time.

The spirituality that has been shared in this meditation is ruthlessly clear on this point. Ecclesial authority is gained by *witness,* ratified by the assent of the community, not by external approbation. No Christian church in the United States has remained free of the sins of racism and sexism. *Toleration* is not a substitute for justice, especially not in the church. While the Black Catholic Church continues its journey toward justice, toward the peaceable kingdom, toward that "great camp-meeting in the promised land," certain ritual behaviors must be displayed to bring us closer to both tolerance and justice. Within the Black Catholic Church system the sisters and daughters and mothers of the church claim their place upon the circle, with as much "authority" as that of any respected elder. Our sons, daughters, mothers, brothers, sisters, and fathers who are lesbian and gay must be blessed and approved as full members of the circle that is church.

To be Catholic is to be inclusive. The circle is formed for the protection of children. If our liturgies, social rituals, and ecclesial structures are not devoted to that principle, then we must be about the rebuilding of the church from the stone floor to the steeple. As the "old lady" (Sr. Thea) was fond of saying, "If it's broke fix it." As this writer is equally fond of saying, "If you (we) are able, you (we) are obligated." We are obligated to reflect in our deliberations and councils the wisdom of a dance-and-song-based culture. One of the greatest tragedies of the failure of leadership in the Black Catholic Church may be the inevitable consequence of raising up leaders and apostolic ministers who felt obligated to "wear the mask" of perfection and super-womanhood and manhood in the face of those who denied us the right to be anywhere in the building, except as servant/slaves. The price we have paid, as a church, as a people, for wearing this mask has been immeasurably high.

Stress-related illnesses; early deaths; addictive behaviors; tragic choices in our personal and professional lives: the stories are a part of our "secret" family history as black Catholics. The stories must also become part of our prophetic witness, to be shared with the young, to be part of our remembering and our reconciliation. And the lives of those so affected, even, at times, lost too early, must be a part of our celebrations. If the masks conceal any truth that can help another to live a better life, then the masks must be discarded.

Rituals of reconciliation cannot be performed across ethnic and "racial" divides when the members of the family cannot join in the ring shout of our deliverance. The history of the Black Catholic Church in the United States is a history of the devoted and heroic laity who maintained a Catholic identity in the face of demonic challenges. The future of the Black Catholic Church will also depend on the laity for its full flowering. The revival of the National Black Catholic Congress movement should be the rallying point for the black Catholic laity to become the harvest of the dream of Daniel Rudd and his fellow delegates at the first congress in 1889. The appointment of more and more black bishops as ordinary episcopal administrators of dioceses in the United States provides a new landscape, one in which culturally based seminary training, strongly protected educational institutions, and a renaissance of religious communities of women are more than examples of wishful thinking.

But none of this will happen, nor will other dreams ever find articulation, until the bishops form a sacred circle and accept the obligation of being members of the family. Following the heroic example of Harold Perry, the first African American bishop ordained in the United States in the twentieth century, the black bishops could very well take up the burden of being, indeed, *black* bishops. During a time of intense pain and promise, Bishop Perry went from place to place being of support and inspiration to black Catholics throughout the United States. It was his policy. Subsequent episcopal appointments have reshaped the vocation to black leadership of many of the men who became bishops after Perry. The pressures of episcopal duties, the complexities of diocesan administration, and the substantial crises these men have had to face in their roles as leaders in the modern urban church have actually rendered many of the bishops seemingly more invisible than Perry ever was.

Each black priest who becomes a bishop could assume a task that will, undoubtedly, be a burden, but one that should be nourished by the attendant grace of the Spirit and the support of a hungry black church. Bishop James P. Lyke assumed leadership of the publication of *Lead Me, Guide Me*. Bishop John H. Ricard assumed leadership of the National Black Catholic Congress and stabilized its reemergence. Each black bishop could, in consultation with those who are able to help him discern his gifts, choose a legacy to contribute to the welfare of the national Black Catholic Church. For one it could be stewardship of educational institutions concerned with the development of lay leadership. For one it could be a devotion to calling forth new communities dedicated to apostolic service. For others it could be the establishment of endowments that would support the work of the "adult" church they symbolize. Some (or all) of them could call for creative programs for training seminarians in culturally appropriate ways and for devising support systems which would ensure their ordination to priestly service. Only with episcopal leadership will there ever be programs designed for the therapeutic care of black priests and religious for whom the stress of apostolic ministry has caused severe illnesses and disabling behaviors.

In order for any of this to happen, the black bishops will have to be lifted up in prayer by the whole African American church, as the gift of prophecy, and of leadership (if not the same gift of martyrdom that was given to Harold Perry), is poured into their souls.

The church must also assemble its prayers on behalf of those who guide us in our liturgical prayer and ritual endeavors. The African American Catholic Church cannot grow into its fullness if there is disunity among its liturgical theologians, ministers of music, and liturgists. And there have been fractures in that circle for decades. How can any be taught how to sit at the welcome table if those in whose care is placed the plans of the sacred banquet are unwilling to sit and pray and laugh and sing with each other? Perhaps it is proof of the existence of the Holy Spirit that contentious musicians can nevertheless lead a congregation in heartfelt and sincere prayer. But this air of contention needs to dissipate and vanish in the Black Catholic Church of today and tomorrow. The witness of being genuinely proud of the accomplishments of each other is a task that all liturgists and church musicians are long overdue in taking up as a part of their ministry. The black bishops recognized that African American Catholic liturgy, properly conceived and well done, is one of the principal methods of evangelization. If black Catholic liturgists cannot sit at the table with each other, anxious to learn from each other, the message that is being sent to the people of God in the pews takes on the flavor of a third-rate daytime drama on television. The liturgy has primacy in our church life. The apostolic work of our liturgical ministers must be valued as highly as possible — both by the ministers themselves and by the people of the church.

My vision tells me that this fractured circle will be healed only when the laity and the bishops join hands with the scholars and the liturgists and lead them to a sacred space where the reconciling dance can be performed.

In one of their most arresting performances, the women's *a capella* singing group Sweet Honey in the Rock proclaims a modern-day Magnificat:

> For each child that's born,
> a morning star rises
> and sings to the universe
> who we are
>
> We are our grandmothers' prayers
> We are our grandfathers' dreamings
> We are the breath of our ancestors
> We are the spirit of God.[20]

All that has been said, in all these pages, is an extended love song to black faith. All men and women born upon this earth can be better than they naturally are. We build upon what we have been given. The glory of the Black Catholic Church in the United States is that no matter the gale-force winds that have assailed it over the last four hundred years, no matter how much interior damage has been done by the squabbling and sibling controversies that have erupted within the church, no matter how deep the gloom and sadness of failure and temporary diminishments of leadership and vision, the church still stands. The song from Sweet Honey in the Rock continues:

> We are
>> Sisters of mercy
>> Brothers of love
>> Lovers of life
>> Builders of nations
>> Seekers of truth
>> Keepers of faith[21]

Let it "resound loud as the rolling sea." Let us picnic in the kingdom of God, setting our welcome table on the rock of our faith.... Let us be church. And so we are. Amen.

Final Meditation

On the day of my ordination to the priesthood, an hour before
       the service began,
I bent before my father's mother and asked her blessing upon
       my life.
The church was filled with saints, angels, the wildly curious and
       deeply grateful.
My father, carrying the sour stone-heavy cancer that would kill
       him, sat waiting.
My mother, my sisters, their children, walked with me to the
       altar.
(My brother husbanded his regrets until we could turn them into
       bread, years later.)
   "Woke up this morning, with my mind stayed on Jesus...."
   "Let my little light shine....Amazing Grace...Here I am
       Lord...."

My mother's mother made the wine that would satisfy us all as
       Jesus (sweet Jesus)
She who taught me all the holy songs, who taught me many of
       the sacred foods,
she was there, a rock in a weary land — soul brimming light-
       spilling joy
   Anybody ask you who you are, who you are,
   Tell them you (my) child of God...and you got a right to
       the tree....
   Are you ready (Certainly Lord) Are you able (Certainly Lord)
   Are you willing (Do, Lord, remember me)

Baptist hymns played by our neighbor, meditations floated by
        St. Louis Jesuits
Mothers of courage held the hands of grandfathers, dreaming;
Sons of promise were carried high by sisters of mercy

Ain't that good news
        Ain't that
Good news good room   in my grandmother's kingdom
Nobody had ever seen a black bishop and a black priest together
So when the stones cried out, the children danced (and played
        basketball and ate too much liberated food)

I sat at the welcome table
Praise God
and you too

Ain't none of us moved yet

March 19, 1997
The Feast of St. Joseph

Notes

Introduction

1. The civilizations contributing most of the influences are studied in Robert Farris Thompson, *Flash of the Spirit: African and Afro-American Art and Philosophy* (New York: Random House, 1983) and in Robert Farris Thompson and Joseph Cornet, *The Four Moments of the Sun: Kongo Art in Two Worlds* (Washington, D.C.: National Gallery of Art, 1981), both of which will be discussed at great length in the text. For the historical context of the Atlantic slave trade, see Basil Davidson, *Africa in History*, rev. ed. (New York: Simon and Schuster, 1991).

2. All scripture references will be taken from the New Revised Standard Version with Apocrypha. Readers are reminded that the foundational texts of African American theology — the songs, sermons, and testimonies — rely on the King James Version of the Bible.

3. Black Catholic Bishops of the United States, *What We Have Seen and Heard: A Pastoral Letter on Evangelization* (Cincinnati: St. Anthony Messenger Press, 1984), 31.

4. Ibid.

Prelude: To Sing the Race

1. W. E. B. Du Bois, *The Souls of Black Folk*, in *W. E. B. Du Bois: Writings* (New York: Library of America, 1986), 495.

2. Revising our perceptions of our cultural ancestors has a special relevance in the age of critical environmental concerns, for example. Affinity with the ecology of the planet is seen as a more sophisticated approach to human respect for the materials of life, as opposed to the solution of technology "at all costs." The "wisdom of the old folks" is no longer the subject of indulgent and patronizing murmurs. What is true of environmental ecological concerns may also be true of many other cultural issues.

3. Countee Cullen, "Yet Do I Marvel," in *Caroling Dusk: An Anthology of Verse by Black Poets*, ed. Countee Cullen (1927; reprint, New York: Citadel Press, 1993), 182.

4. Du Bois, *Souls*, 539.

Chapter 1: Wheels within Wheels

1. A succinct summary of the shift in anthropological analysis and a pertinent commentary on some of the themes of the present study can be found in Walter Ong, "African Talking Drums," in his *Interfaces of the Word* (Ithaca, N.Y.: Cornell University Press, 1977), 92–120.

2. Olaudah Equiano, "The Interesting Narrative of the Life of Olaudah Equiano," in *The Classic Slave Narratives*, ed. Henry Louis Gates Jr. (New York: Mentor Books, 1987), 14.

3. General Oglethorpe to the accountant, Mr. Harmon Verelst, quoted in Dena J. Epstein, *Sinful Tunes and Spirituals: Black Folk Music to the Civil War* (Urbana: University of Illinois Press, 1977), 40.

4. Nearly one hundred years later, Thomas Jefferson prophesied that the eventual outcome of African enslavement would be the production of "convulsions which will probably never end but in the extermination of one or the other race" (Thomas Jefferson, *Notes on the State of Virginia*, query 14, in *Writings* [New York: Library of America, 1984], 264). Jefferson's dire nightmare, which caused him to "tremble" when he considered that God was just, gave heart and hope to one of his most eloquent critics. In his *Appeal to the Colored Citizens of the World...* (1829; reprint, New York: Hill and Wang, 1965), David Walker uses the Stono Rebellion and similar acts of rebellion to call on black Americans to use even bloody acts of liberation as instruments of God's justice. Some would speculate that Nat Turner followed such exhortations a few years later. David Brion Davis, in *The Slave Power Conspiracy and the Paranoid Style* (Baton Rouge: Louisiana State University Press, 1982), shows how pro-slavery state governments (or, more accurately, *antiblack* governments) throughout the United States built a universe of laws upon the widespread fear of the annihilation of whites by blacks. The effects of many of these laws — and the mind-set that created them — are still present in American culture.

5. Epstein, *Sinful Tunes*.

6. Robert Farris Thompson, "An Aesthetic of the Cool: West African Dance," in *The Theater of Black Americans*, vol. 1: *Roots and Rituals/The Image Makers*, ed. Errol Hill (Englewood Cliffs, N.J.: Prentice-Hall, 1980), 99. Thompson adapts and elaborates this paradigm in the introduction to his *Flash of the Spirit* (New York: Random House: 1983), xiii. Both versions of his elaboration will be utilized here.

7. Thompson, "Aesthetic," 109. Thompson uses this insight as the basis for much of his most ground-breaking analysis of all forms of African and African American visual art. From his analysis of art, he derives a far-reaching philosophy of African and African American living and creativity. His insights are leaven for those who read him.

8. Robert Farris Thompson and Joseph Cornet, *The Four Moments of the Sun: Kongo Art in Two Worlds* (Washington, D.C.: National Gallery of Art, 1981), 44, 43.

9. Kimpianga Mahaniah, quoted in ibid., 95.

10. John Miller Chernoff, *African Rhythm and African Sensibility* (Chicago: University of Chicago Press, 1979), 150.

11. Equiano, "Interesting Narrative," 22.

12. Joseph M. Murphy, *Working the Spirit: Ceremonies of the African Diaspora* (Boston: Beacon Press, 1993), 180. Murphy offers many wise observations on the ritual continuities of African culture on both sides of the Atlantic.

13. Chernoff, *African Rhythm*, 144. In this passage, Chernoff makes a reference to Thompson's "Aesthetic of the Cool."

14. Bernard McGinn, *The Foundations of Mysticism: Origins to the Fifth Century* (New York: Crossroad, 1995), xvii. The same description, as we have seen, can be found in the work of Robert Farris Thompson, Dominique Zahan, and others, most especially Zora Neale Hurston, who will be discussed in later chapters.

15. McGinn, *Foundations*, xvii.

16. Thompson, *Flash*, 5.

17. Henry John Drewal and John Pemberton III, with Rowland Abiodun, *Yoruba: Nine Centuries of African Art and Thought* (New York: Harry Abrams, 1989), 16.

18. Dominique Zahan, *The Religion, Spirituality, and Thought of Traditional Africa* (Chicago: University of Chicago Press, 1979), 4.

19. McGinn, *Foundations*, 135.

20. Zahan, *Religion*, 15. The reader is advised to correct Zahan's gender-specific prose wherever appropriate. Certain issues of typographic translation are obvious to both reader and writer.

21. Ibid., 17.

22. Examples of such rendering of mystics in European art can be found in E. H. Gombrich, *The Story of Art* (London: Phaidon Press, 1995). The plates of Corregio's *The Holy Night* (336) and Bernini's *The Ecstasy of St. Teresa* (439) are remarkably clear. However, no discussion of African art is present in the text, suggesting that the book is, rather, "the story of *some* art."

23. Joseph Conrad, *Heart of Darkness*, in *Heart of Darkness and Other Stories* (Oxford: Oxford University Press, 1990), 225. This passage must be forever linked with the brilliant and forceful challenge to Conrad presented by Chinua Achebe in "An Image of Africa," in *Chant of Saints*, ed. Michael S. Harper and Robert B. Stepto (Urbana: University of Illinois Press, 1979), 313-25.

24. D. H. Lawrence, *Women in Love* (1920; reprint, New York: Penguin Books, 1979), 71.

25. Gertrude Stein, *Picasso* (1938; reprint, New York: Dover, 1984), passim. These comments come from a woman who dismissed Paul Robeson for his singing of Negro spirituals, asserting that Robeson was engaged

in futility in arguing for the spirituals' cultural importance. "The negro suffers from nothingness," Ms. Stein famously said. She also admitted that she learned her repetitive style of writing from listening to Negro speech while serving as a midwife in Baltimore in the late 1890s. Stein's problematic dependence on African American aesthetics for her own narrative style is fully discussed in my "Harmonic Circles: Afro-American Religious Heritage and American Aesthetics" (Ph.D. diss., Yale University, 1984), 181–87.

26. Robert Farris Thompson, *African Art in Motion: Icon and Act* (Washington, D.C: National Gallery of Art, 1974), xiv.

27. Aylward Shorter, in *Jesus and the Witchdoctor* (Maryknoll, N.Y.: Orbis Books, 1985), provides a contemporary reading of this phenomenon and displays an understanding of traditional healing that is refreshingly devoid of prejudice and sentimentalism.

Chapter 2: How Does It Feel to Come Out the Wilderness?

1. Vincent Harding, *There Is a River: The Black Struggle for Freedom in America* (New York: Random House, 1983), 15–23; emphasis added.

2. Ibid. John Blassingame, in *The Slave Community: Plantation Life in the Antebellum South,* rev. and enlarged ed. (New York: Oxford University Press, 1979), makes the same point about suicides, adding: "Often they committed suicide (especially while still on the African coast) by drowning, or refusing food or medicine, rather than accept enslavement" (7).

3. Miles Mark Fisher, in *Negro Slave Songs in the United States* (New York: Citadel Press, 1953), did recognize the code of *Africa* in all of the *water* and *river* songs. Unfortunately, he fell victim to a narrow interpretation that did not permit any sense of transcendence or inclusion of biblical theology. For Fisher, every slave song referred to political organizing and responses to the movement of the African Colonization Society. No interpretation of the spirituals can rely on *binary* theories of "either/or" descriptions. As in all true art, multiple layers of symbolism and meaning reside in the spirituals.

4. Howard W. Odum and Guy B. Johnson, *The Negro and His Songs* (1925; reprint, New York: New American Library, 1969), 141. It would be safe to remark that the surviving Africans who saw their sisters and brothers end their mortal lives in the waters also saw the schools of sharks that followed the vessels and handed on that memory also. Harding makes this comment in *River,* 18.

5. Harding, *River,* 19.

6. James H. Cone, *The Spirituals and the Blues* (New York: Seabury Press, 1972), 5.

7. James Weldon Johnson and J. Rosamund Johnson, *The Books of American Negro Spirituals,* 2 vols. (1925, 1926; reprint, New York: Da Capo Press, 1977), 2:12. The prefaces contained in this collection of spirituals should rank with the sections of W. E. B. Du Bois's *The Souls of*

Black Folk, in *W. E. B. Du Bois: Writings* (New York: Library of America, 1986), as exemplary of the best African American cultural studies based on sacred music.

8. Robert Farris Thompson and Joseph Cornet, *The Four Moments of the Sun: Kongo Art in Two Worlds* (Washington, D.C.: National Gallery of Art, 1981), 44, 43.

9. Olaudah Equiano, "The Interesting Narrative of the Life of Olaudah Equiano," in *The Classic Slave Narratives,* ed. Henry Louis Gates Jr. (New York: Mentor Books, 1987), 14. The term "slave narratives" has been placed within quotation marks in the text because it seems a highly inappropriate label, explaining quite a bit less than is intended by the usage of the term. The texts are documents of *liberation* and should be known as such. (In the same way, Du Bois's naming of the spirituals as the "sorrow songs" also confuses more than enlightens — since many of the songs deal with triumph and victory and are too spirited and lively in their composition and execution to be simply considered the songs of an "unhappy people.") The need to impose political labels from without is so common as to be an invincible tendency, as far as this study is concerned. At least the protest can be registered. The use of appropriate language — language that represents the intentions of the *subjects* — should be a goal whenever and wherever possible.

10. Frederick Douglass, *Narrative of the Life of Frederick Douglass, an American Slave: Written by Himself,* ed. Benjamin Quarles (Cambridge, Mass.: Belknap Press, 1960), 36.

11. Ibid., 37. Douglass, at the height of a rhetorical crest, loses his earlier insight: the songs reveal the highest joy and the deepest sorrow — simultaneously. If Du Bois and other students of Douglass had performed a multivalent reading of the songs, as opposed to narrowly conceiving them as songs of sorrow and unhappiness, then African American culture might have been spared the unbalanced emphasis on the pathology of slavery, often ignoring the human triumphs of a people singing themselves from the gates of hell to the golden streets of heaven.

12. This last consideration challenges many of the prevailing aesthetic theories, most notably deconstruction and its progeny. If, as this study maintains, the originating artists of African American culture were self-consciously creating an art that would haunt, disturb, and restructure the epistemology of slavery; and if that art is handed down as a legacy and sacred trust to each new generation, then any theory of art that limits or denies the intentions of the artists themselves will be in conflict with any authentic African American aesthetic.

13. A quick survey of such observations can be found in Eugene Genovese, *Roll, Jordan, Roll* (New York: Vintage Books, 1976), especially in the chapter "The Gospel in the Quarters" (248–52). Other observers' reactions

can be found in Bernard Katz, ed., *The Social Implications of Early Negro Music in America* (New York: Arno Press, 1960).

14. Blassingame, *Slave Community*, 310–11.

15. Thompson, *Flash*, 117.

16. Ibid.

17. The Kongo cosmogram is discussed at great length in ibid. and also in Thompson and Cornet, *Four Moments*.

18. Thompson, *Flash*, 121.

19. Such an "accident" would be a much more positive attribution than that found in Thomas Jefferson's gratuitous dismissal of Phillis Wheatley's poetry and, by a small extension, his denial of Africans' and African Americans' abilities to write poetry. Even in his condescension, though, Jefferson was able to perceive that the religious impulse of African and African American art was present from the beginning. "Among the blacks is misery enough, God knows, but no poetry. Love is the peculiar oestrum of the poet. Their love is ardent, but it kindles the senses only, not the imagination. Religion indeed has produced a Phyllis Whately [sic]; but it could not produce a poet" (Thomas Jefferson, *Writings* [New York: Library of America, 1984], 267).

20. T. W. Higginson, *Army Life in a Black Regiment* (New York: W. W. Norton, 1984), 212.

21. Ibid., 233. So, perhaps, the textual emendation from "gird on the armor" to "guide on the army" might have been due to a decision that *armor* was an archaic image, while that of warrior-angels leading the divinely appointed avenging host was more apt.

22. Dudley Taylor Cornish, *The Sable Arm: Black Troops in the Union Army, 1861–1865* (Lawrence: University Press of Kansas, 1987), 273–74.

23. Morrison uses this phrase as a eulogy spoken by Milkman, upon the death of his aunt, Pilate, at the conclusion of *Song of Solomon* (New York: Alfred A. Knopf, 1977), 336.

24. Higginson, *Army Life*, 41.

25. Ibid. Eileen Southern provides other descriptions in *The Music of Black Americans* (New York: W. W. Norton, 1971), 160–63. Du Bois's famous description in *The Souls of Black Folk* (493) and the descriptions found in Fisher's *Negro Slave Songs* echo, sometimes verbatim, the descriptions in *Army Life*. The closest echo of Higginson's observations are found in William Francis Allen et al., eds., *Slave Songs of the United States* (1867; reprint, New York: Dover, 1995).

26. Higginson, *Army Life*, 41.

27. Northrup Frye, *The Great Code: The Bible and Literature* (Toronto: Academic Press Canada, 1982), 31–32.

28. "Kerygma," in *Our Sunday Visitor's Catholic Encyclopedia* (Huntington, Ind.: Our Sunday Visitor Press, 1991), 553.

29. From among the dozens of studies of the revival movement and the development of the spiritualist churches in African and African American communities the following references might be helpful to those who would appreciate further information on this phenomenon: Hans A. Baer, *The Black Spiritualist Movement: A Religious Response to Racism* (Knoxville: University of Tennessee Press, 1984); Jason Berry, *The Spirit of Black Hawk: A Mystery of Africans and Indians* (Jackson: University Press of Mississippi, 1995); and Donald G. Mathews, *Religion in the Old South* (Chicago: University of Chicago Press, 1979).

Second Meditation: Climbing Jacob's Ladder

1. T. W. Higginson, *Army Life in a Black Regiment* (New York: W. W. Norton, 1984), 199–200.

2. This telling of the story of Jacob is the centerpiece of this study. The "African" and the "Christian" are blended through the mystical insights of African American spirituality. It has long struck me as odd that Sigmund Freud found myths aplenty for his analysis of id, ego, and superego, of identity, neurosis, and dream interpretations in a culture that came to him secondarily. The great Hebrew stories that are also the common heritage of so many of the peoples of the world are rich repositories of myths that would enlighten these theories, and many others. For the version of the story that I have shared here, two other icons of modernism are principally invoked. The model of the story derives its shape from the story of Abraham that begins Søren Kierkegaard's *Fear and Trembling* (New York: Penguin Books, 1985). Some of the interpretations of the inner struggle of Jacob gain their texture from my repeated reading of Thomas Mann's masterwork, the tetralogy, *Joseph and His Brothers* (New York: Alfred A. Knopf, 1974).

3. Thomas Jefferson, *Notes on the State of Virginia,* query 18, in *Writings* (New York: Library of America, 1984), 289.

4. Abraham Lincoln, *Speeches and Writings: 1859–65* (New York: Library of America, 1989), 686.

5. James Baldwin, introduction to *The Price of the Ticket: Collected Nonfiction 1948–1985* (New York: St. Martin's/Marek, 1985), xx.

Chapter 3: To Go in the Wilderness

1. The most important thinkers in these areas are discussed with great competence in David Brion Davis, *The Problem of Slavery in the Age of Revolution: 1770–1823* (Ithaca, N.Y.: Cornell University Press, 1975); in John C. Greene, *The Death of Adam: Evolution and Its Impact on Western Thought* (Ames: Iowa State University Press, 1974); and in Winthrop D. Jordan, *White over Black: American Attitudes toward the Negro, 1550–1812* (New York: W. W. Norton, 1977).

2. Walt Whitman, "Letter to Ralph Waldo Emerson," in *Leaves of Grass, 1856*, in *Walt Whitman: The Complete Poems* (Baltimore: Penguin Education, 1975), 765.

3. Jean Toomer, "Song of the Son," in *Cane* (1923; reprint, New York: Liveright, 1975), 12.

4. Sources which discuss these and other collectors of culture can be found in Eileen Southern, *The Music of Black Americans* (New York: W. W. Norton, 1971), especially in her bibliography; in Lawrence Levine, *Black Culture and Black Consciousness* (New York: Oxford University Press, 1977), which also provides a wealth of bibliographic suggestions; and in George P. Rawick, ed., *The American Slave: A Composite Autobiography*, 20 vols. (Westport: Greenwood, 1972), a collection of the interviews with the former enslaved.

5. Most of the authors just cited, and many other representative efforts to provide a model of how the past and the present should be blended, can be found in Alain Locke, ed., *The New Negro: Voices of the Harlem Renaissance* (1925; reprint, New York: Atheneum, 1992).

6. In addition to the previously cited work of James Baldwin, two studies are important resources for the themes presented here. Toni Morrison, in *Playing in the Dark: Whiteness and the Literary Imagination* (Cambridge, Mass.: Harvard University Press, 1992), demands that our gaze remain unwavering in our confrontation with what has stayed unspoken for far too long in literary and cultural criticism. Eric Lott, in *Love and Theft: Blackface Minstrelsy and the American Working Class* (New York: Oxford University Press, 1995), provides a brilliant overview of the importance of the blackface minstrel tradition in establishing the popular parameters of blackness/whiteness in the nineteenth and early twentieth centuries. The resurgence of the minstrel tradition in the genre of hip-hop music and fashion needs the same deep reading.

7. A wise way of reading history with a sense of inclusion is found in the work of Ronald Takaki, especially his *A Different Mirror: A History of Multicultural America* (Boston: Little, Brown, 1993). One of the more entertaining studies of the peculiar twists by which history gets rewritten without much consistent reflection is found in Kenneth S. Greenberg, *Honor and Slavery* (Princeton, N.J.: Princeton University Press, 1996), which focuses on the language and behavior of white southern males before the Civil War.

8. James Weldon Johnson and J. Rosamund Johnson, "Lift Ev'ry Voice and Sing," in *Lead Me, Guide Me: The African American Catholic Hymnal* (Chicago: G. I. A. Publications, Inc., 1987), no. 291.

9. As told in Arthur C. Jones, *Wade in the Water: The Wisdom of the Spirituals* (Maryknoll, N.Y.: Orbis Books, 1993), 123.

10. The great historical issues are magisterially displayed in W. E. B. Du Bois, *Black Reconstruction in America: 1860–1880* (New York: Athe-

neum, 1935). A general review of these times can be found in John Hope Franklin and Alfred A. Moss Jr., *From Slavery to Freedom: A History of African Americans,* 7th ed. (New York: McGraw-Hill, 1994).

11. W. E. B. Du Bois, *The Souls of Black Folk,* in *W. E. B. Du Bois: Writings* (New York: Library of America, 1986).

12. This widespread belief in the power derived from birth order and the retention of the placenta is universally understood in the African American communities. It is succinctly reported in Albert Raboteau, *Slave Religion* (New York: Oxford University Press, 1978), 276. Another reading of this passage, depending on a radically different understanding of spirituality and mysticism, can be found in Cynthia D. Schrager, "Both Sides of the Veil: Race, Science and Mysticism in W. E. B. Du Bois," *American Quarterly* 48, no. 4 (December 1996): 551.

13. For anyone who would need a more complete understanding of the most complex of terms, *signifying,* I would suggest the exhaustive and comprehensive study by Henry Louis Gates Jr., *The Signifying Monkey: A Theory of African American Literary Criticism* (New York: Oxford University Press, 1988), esp. 72–78. Especially helpful is Gates's suggestion that one meaning of signification can be considered "linguistic masking, the verbal sign of the mask of blackness that demarcates the boundary between the white linguistic realm and the black, two domains that exist side by side in a homonymic relation" (77).

14. W. E. B. Du Bois, "Dusk of Dawn," in *Writings,* 570. Cullen's poem can be found in Locke, ed., *New Negro,* 250.

15. Du Bois, "Dusk of Dawn," 640.

16. One of the many places where Du Bois weighs in against the "great invention of race" can be found in his essay "The Conservation of Races," in *Writings,* 815.

17. Gwendolyn Brooks, "The Sermon on the Warpland," from *In the Mecca,* in *The World of Gwendolyn Brooks* (New York: Harper and Row, 1971), 421.

18. Ibid., 426.

19. "Me and My Captain," in *The Norton Anthology of African American Literature,* ed. Henry Louis Gates Jr. and Nellie Y. McKay (New York: W. W. Norton, 1997), 38.

20. A basic reading of the meaning of "sacramental" could be of help here. One definition is: "Sacred signs, bearing a certain likeness to the sacraments, by which spiritual effects are signified and obtained by the intercession of the Church. Some sacramentals are objects;...others are actions" ("Sacramentals," in *Our Sunday Visitor's Catholic Encyclopedia* [Huntington, Ind.: Our Sunday Visitor Books, 1991], 848). Vatican II's Constitution on the Sacred Liturgy adds a comment to this basic understanding that is worth noting here: "There is hardly any proper use of material things which cannot thus be directed toward the sanctification of

men and the praise of God" (in *The Documents of Vatican II*, ed. Walter M. Abbott, S.J. [New York: Association Press, 1966], 158 [no. 61]).

21. James Weldon Johnson and J. Rosamund Johnson, *The Books of American Negro Spirituals*, 2 vols. (1925, 1926; reprint, New York: Da Capo Press, 1977), 1:71

22. John Blassingame provides, as editor, many stories of such persecutions in his *Slave Testimony: Two Centuries of Letters, Speeches, Interviews, and Autobiographies* (Baton Rouge: Louisiana State University Press, 1977). Each of the narratives collected by Henry Louis Gates Jr. in *The Classic Slave Narratives* (New York: Mentor Books, 1987) also contains stories of religious intolerance. And, of course, the final chapter of the first autobiography of Frederick Douglass, *Narrative of the Life of Frederick Douglass, an American Slave: Written by Himself* (in *Classic Slave Narratives*), contains his argument against "slaveholding Christianity," one of the most powerful indictments of hypocrisy in organized religion to be found in American literature.

23. "Sit Down, Servant," arranged by Margaret Bonds, sung by Leontyne Price, on *Leontyne Price: Swing Low, Sweet Chariot: Fourteen Spirituals* (RCA LSC 2600. 1962).

Interlude: Steal Away to Jesus

1. Albert Raboteau, *Slave Religion* (New York: Oxford University Press, 1978), 214, 219.

Chapter 4: Sometimes I Feel Like a Motherless Child

1. First and foremost is the work of Cyprian Davis, O.S.B., in his *The History of Black Catholics in the United States* (New York: Crossroad, 1991). Albert J. Raboteau writes of black Catholic history, both in *Slave Religion* (New York: Oxford University Press, 1978) and in *A Fire in the Bones* (Boston: Beacon Press, 1995). Giles A. Conwill provides a succinct and challenging overview of the history of black Catholics in the United States in his essay "Can These Bones Live?" which appears in *'Rise 'N' Shine: Catholic Education and the African American Community*, ed. Sr. Mary Alice Chineworth, O.S.P. (Washington, D.C.: National Catholic Educational Association, 1996).

2. Davis, *History*, 40. The chapter in which these comments appear, "A Church in Chains," is as fine a picture as can be easily found of the economic value accruing to Roman Catholic establishments from the use of enslaved labor (and the occasional sale of enslaved men and women).

3. Ibid., 21–23.

4. Ignatius of Loyola, *The Autobiography of St. Ignatius Loyola*, trans. Joseph F. O'Callaghan, ed. John C. Olin (New York: Harper and Row, 1974), 30.

5. The grand irony of this situation cannot be overlooked. The shrine at Montserrat was dedicated to one of the more famous images of the black Madonna to be found in all of Europe. La Morenata, the "little black Madonna," has been the focus of Christian reverence and devotion since the eighth century.

6. Kenneth P. Feit, "St. Louis Area Jesuits and the Interracial Apostolate, 1823–1969" (M.A. thesis, St. Louis University, 1969). Feit and this author were classmates at St. Louis University at the time of the writing of this thesis; at the time Feit was a member of the Society of Jesus.

7. Edward F. Beckett, S.J., "Listening to Our History: Inculturation and Jesuit Slaveholding," *Studies in the Spirituality of Jesuits* 28, no. 5 (1996): 36.

8. The negative attributes shackled to Africans, enslaved or otherwise, which are summarized here have been distilled from the following authors. Most informative is Winthrop D. Jordan, *White over Black: American Attitudes toward the Negro, 1550–1812* (New York: W. W. Norton, 1968). Also of great insight are John Blassingame, *The Slave Community: Plantation Life in the Antebellum South*, rev. and enlarged ed. (New York: Oxford University Press, 1979); David Brion Davis, *The Problem of Slavery in Western Culture* (Ithaca, N.Y.: Cornell University Press, 1966); idem, *The Problem of Slavery in the Age of Revolution, 1770–1823* (Ithaca, N.Y.: Cornell University Press, 1975); and Ronald Summers, *Lost Tribes and Promised Lands* (Boston: Little, Brown, 1978). In *North of Slavery: The Negro in the Free States, 1790–1860* (Chicago: University of Chicago Press, 1961), Leon F. Litwack proves that theories of racial inferiority were not bounded by geography or social status in the United States.

9. Robert E. Hood, *Begrimed and Black: Christian Traditions on Blacks and Blackness* (Minneapolis: Fortress Press, 1994), 79. Hood's study should be required reading in every seminary and school where clerical and religious formation is conducted for Christians in the United States. The pervasive quality of such racialist thinking often makes efforts to isolate and challenge racist assumptions very difficult. Hood is especially helpful in showing how the "virus of racism" (my term) has infected African Americans when we reflect on our own spiritual qualities. Winthrop D. Jordan's *White over Black* remains the standard reference for the study of this topic.

10. Hood, *Begrimed*, 87–97.

11. In addition to the comments found throughout Jordan's *White over Black*, the reader would benefit from Blassingame, *Slave Community*. Writers from Nathaniel Hawthorne to Norman Mailer, and from Harriet Jacobs (Linda Brent) to Toni Morrison, have produced significant literature concerning white obsession with black sexuality.

12. Hood, *Begrimed*, 149.

13. Ibid., 149–50. This fascination continued well into the twentieth century and was not reserved to black males. In the nineteenth century,

the most famous, and most gruesome, castration was probably the genital castration and preservation in a museum of the sexual organs of the African woman known as the "Venus Hottentot." See Saundra Sharp, *Black Women for Beginners*, illustrated by Beverly Hawkins Hall (New York: Writers and Readers, 1993), 75.

14. A thorough discussion of the "other" in European discourse can be found in Abdul R. JanMohamed, "The Economy of Manichean Allegory: The Function of Racial Difference in Colonialist Literature," in *"Race," Writing, and Difference,* ed. Henry Louis Gates Jr. (Chicago: University of Chicago Press, 1985), 78–106.

15. The biographical information (chronology and memoirs) found in *Sister Thea Bowman, Shooting Star: Selected Writings and Speeches,* ed. Sr. Celestine Cepress, F.S.P.A. (Winona, Ind.: St. Mary's Press, 1993) is invaluable for providing the proper context alluded to here.

16. For the purposes of the study engaged here, two references will adequately represent the vast scholarship that seeks to explain these divisions within the Christian world. Huston Smith, *The World's Religions* (San Francisco: HarperSanFrancisco, 1991), 356–63, offers a clear, general summary of the principles of Protestantism that are of importance to us presently. Sydney E. Ahlstrom, *A Religious History of the American People,* vol. 1 (Garden City, N.Y.: Doubleday Image, 1975), presents a dramatic and compelling account of the evangelical fire that burned the souls of thousands of Africans in America from 1620 to 1860.

17. Ahlstrom, *Religious History,* 396ff.

18. Frederick Douglass spelled out his eloquent brief against hypocrisy in the churches at the end of *Narrative of the Life of Frederick Douglass, an American Slave: Written by Himself* (in *Classic Slave Narratives,* ed. Henry Louis Gates Jr. [New York: Mentor Books, 1987]), in the appendix. Douglass added his voice to a chorus of black Jeremiahs, the most notable of whom was David Walker, who outlined the apocalyptic judgments awaiting the "false churches" of America in *David Walker's Appeal to the Colored Citizens of the World...* (1829; reprint, New York: Hill and Wang, 1965).

19. Raboteau details this glorious period of black church history in *Slave Religion* and in *A Fire in the Bones.*

20. From Richard Allen, *The Life Experience and Gospel Labors of the Rt. Rev. Richard Allen (1833),* quoted in Milton C. Sernett, ed., *Afro-American Religious History: A Documentary Witness* (Chapel Hill, N.C.: Duke University Press, 1985), 143.

21. Ibid., 145.

22. Joseph M. Davis, "Reflections on a Central Office for Black Catholicism," *Freeing the Spirit* 3, no. 1 (1972), cited in John Michael Spencer, ed., *Black Hymnody: A Hymnological History of the African-American Church* (Knoxville: University of Tennessee Press, 1992), 198. Spencer's study of the history of the black church through its music is a first-rate and long

overdue approach. His chapter entitled "The Roman Catholic Church," from which the Davis comments were taken, is perhaps the best review, so far, of the black Catholic liturgical movement of the late twentieth century.

23. Some historians and critics have begun to weigh in with less and less hesitation concerning the seemingly willful contradictions Jefferson displayed in his ideas on race. For an especially provocative interpretation of Thomas Jefferson's supposed racism, see Conor Cruise O'Brien, "Thomas Jefferson: Radical and Racist," *Atlantic Monthly* 278, no. 4 (October 1996): 53–74.

24. Thomas Jefferson, *Writings* (New York: Library of America, 1984), 265. The passage quoted here continues on, in a similar vein. Jefferson's comments could be interpreted as supremely silly, if not for the fact that his close contact with the horrors of slavery, detailed elsewhere in the same book, only underscores his rhetorical hypocrisy.

25. George Brown Tindall, with David E. Shi, *America: A Narrative History*, 3d ed. (New York: W. W. Norton, 1988), 2:720.

26. Ibid., 747.

27. George M. Fredrickson, *The Arrogance of Race* (Middletown, Conn.: Wesleyan University Press, 1989), 176. These comments appear as part of a review of Joel Williamson's *The Crucible of Race: Black–White Relations in the American South since Emancipation* (New York: Oxford University Press, 1984).

28. Mary Frances Berry and John W. Blassingame, *Long Memory: The Black Experience in America* (New York: Oxford University Press, 1982), 122. It is somewhat curious that these two black historians devote as much time as they do to the issue of voluntary interracial sexual contact in their discussion of lynching and the other forms of organized terror inflicted upon African Americans and upon their white friends, associates, and advocates. It is, at the same time, refreshing that Berry and Blassingame see the need to air out some of the pathological ghosts in the closets of the American psyche. Too often the memories are not "long," but "suppressed."

29. Father Clarence Joseph Rivers is the founding prophet of the modern liturgical movement in the Black Catholic Church (and in the Roman Catholic Church in the United States in general). His ideas have a significant influence on the remainder of this book.

30. A loving portrait of the heroic endeavors of these and other likeminded African American women can be found in Davis, *History*, 98–115.

31. Marie-Jeanne Aliquot, a white woman native to France, dedicated her life to work among black people and is considered by the Sisters of the Holy Family as a member of their foundation, even though the laws of the time prohibited an integrated community.

32. Mother Mary Bernard Deggs, "Journal," transcribed by Virginia Meacham Gould and Charles E. Nolan (1995–96), 25. These comments and those that follow are taken from the manuscript, which is still in prepa-

ration for its final form. I was most graciously given an opportunity to study this manuscript, with a view of commenting upon some of the theology found in its pages. When the "Journal" is ready for publication, the whole genre of black women's narratives in the nineteenth century will have to be adjusted to make room for this astonishing text.

33. Collected in *Classic Slave Narratives,* ed. Gates.

34. In 1989, George A. Stallings Jr., then a diocesan priest serving in the archdiocese of Washington, D.C., established the Imani Temple as the cornerstone of his "African American Catholic Congregation." Since then other African Americans, some of them prominent representatives of the black Catholic clerical, religious, and lay communities, have joined Stallings's movement. Cyprian Davis discusses this movement in the postscript to his *History,* 260. In 1997, Marist Brother Cyprian L. Rowe, one of the founders of the National Black Catholic Clergy Caucus and a prominent black Catholic intellectual, defected to the AACC. This is discussed in a Catholic News Service article in the *Clarion Herald* (archdiocese of New Orleans, February 20, 1997), 8.

35. Stephen J. Ochs, *Desegregating the Altar: The Josephites and the Struggle for Black Priests, 1871–1960* (Baton Rouge: Louisiana State University Press, 1990), 81.

36. Ibid., 93.

37. Ibid., 40.

38. Ibid., 94.

39. Lawrence E. Lucas, *Black Priest, White Church* (New York: Random House, 1970).

40. Ralph Ellison, *Invisible Man,* 2d international ed. (New York: Random House, 1995), 572, 573.

41. Ibid., 573.

42. Kendall Thomas, " 'Ain't Nothin' Like the Real Thing': Black Masculinity, Gay Sexuality, and the Jargon of Authenticity," in *The House That Race Built: Black Americans, U.S. Terrain,* ed. Wahneema Lubiano (New York: Pantheon Books, 1997), 126.

43. Ellis Cose, *The Rage of a Privileged Class* (New York: HarperCollins, 1993), 189. Cose, a senior editor at *Newsweek* magazine, has complemented this study of the frustrations facing the black middle class with a masterful reflection on "where do we go from here," in *Color-Blind: Seeing beyond Race in a Race-Obsessed World* (New York: HarperCollins, 1997).

44. Toni Morrison explores these alternative themes in her essay "Home," which appears in *The House That Race Built,* ed. Lubiano, 3–12.

Chapter 5: Plenty Good Room in the Kingdom

1. Bernice Johnson Reagon, *The Songs Are Free* (New York: Mystic Fire Videos, 1991), a conversation with Bill Moyers. This illuminating and

nourishing documentary on the work of Bernice Reagon clearly demonstrates the value of the traditional songs and the spirit of renewal in the continuous production of black sacred songs. All subsequent comments in this text from Reagon are found in this video presentation.

2. Albert J. Raboteau, *Slave Religion* (New York: Oxford University Press, 1978), 246.

3. Toni Morrison, *Beloved* (New York: NAL Penguin, 1987), 87. All subsequent references to this work are noted in the text.

4. Sr. Thea Bowman, *Sister Thea Bowman, Shooting Star: Selected Writings and Speeches,* ed. Sr. Celestine Cepress, F.S.P.A. (Winona, Ind.: St. Mary's Press, 1993), 32. The dynamics of a "culture of pathology" would include the sense that African Americans are "culturally" deficient; inferior; lacking in an appreciation for the components of the "Protestant work ethic" (e.g., punctuality, thrift, personal responsibility); unable to appreciate traditional "family values"; prone to violence and to addictive behaviors. These (and other factors attributed to "the permanent underclass") demand that societal forces offer instruction, charity, discipline, and surveillance to African Americans whoever and wherever they are. It should be obvious that I reject such a cultural reading of African American experience.

5. Wyatt Tee Walker, *"Somebody's Calling My Name,"* cited in Arthur C. Jones, *Wade in the Water: The Wisdom of the Spirituals* (Maryknoll, N.Y.: Orbis Books, 1993), 130.

6. This analysis, from *The Songs Are Free,* also appears in Jones, *Wade in the Water,* 22.

7. Ibid.

8. In *The Songs Are Free;* and also in Jones, *Wade in the Water,* 129.

9. Ibid.

10. Bowman, *Shooting Star,* 32; subsequent references to this work are given in the text.

11. Audre Lorde, *Sister Outsider* (Trumansburg, N.Y.: The Crossing Press, 1984), 42–43. This quotation served as a foundation for my essay "This Little Light of Mine: The Possibility of Prophecy in the Black Catholic Church," which was written in honor of Thea Bowman and which appears in *Thea Bowman: Handing on Her Legacy,* ed. Christian Koontz (Kansas City: Sheed and Ward, 1991).

12. Constitution on the Sacred Liturgy, in *The Documents of Vatican II,* ed. Walter M. Abbott, S.J. (New York: Association Press, 1966), 142 (no. 10).

13. Ibid., 143.

14. Clarence Joseph Rivers, *Soulfull Worship* (Cincinnati: Stimuli, 1974), 20.

15. Music from each of the aforementioned artists and musical styles can be found in the great jewel of black Catholic liturgical development,

Lead Me, Guide Me: The African American Catholic Hymnal, which was published in 1987, just a few years after the pastoral letter, *What We Have Seen and Heard* (1984). These two texts appeared a decade after the foundational work of Clarence Rivers, *Soulfull Worship* (1974), and *This Far by Faith* (Washington, D.C.: National Office of Black Catholics and the Liturgical Conference, 1977).

The founding of the Institute for Black Catholic Studies (in 1980) and the restoration of the National Black Catholic Congress movement (in 1987) in the next decade spoke to the need to build institutions that could help black Catholics to reclaim their history and to define their own future.

16. J-Glenn Murray, S.J., "The Remembering Community," *Plenty Good Room* (Chicago: Liturgy Training Publications) 3, no. 2 (November 1995): 8. Murray has been an active consultant for the *Lead Me, Guide Me* project and for many of the publications sponsored by the Black Secretariat of the United States Catholic Conference; and he is the founding editor of *Plenty Good Room,* which began publication in 1993, continuing the tradition started by the National Office of Black Catholics in the late 1960s.

17. Rivers, *Soulfull Worship,* 21.

18. The political and economic imposition of *categories of race* has produced more confusion than clarity. It is the "price of the ticket," as James Baldwin has told us. No person can claim a "pure" racial identity, and the laws, customs, and suppositions that bolster such false claims constitute systematic racism. Every human being is "multicultural" by virtue of being born.

19. Among his generation of cultural critics, Michael Eric Dyson seems particularly insightful in his analysis of these concerns. See his *Race Rules: Navigating the Color Line* (Reading, Mass.: Addison-Wesley, 1996).

20. "We Are," words and music, by Yaye M. Barnwell (1993), on *Sweet Honey in the Rock: Sacred Ground* (EarthBeat Records, 1995).

21. Ibid.

Index